1-2-3 Magic

Effective Discipline for Children 2-12

1-2-3 Magic

Thomas W. Phelan, Ph.D.

CHILD MANAGEMENT INC

Glen Ellyn, Illinois

Cover design and illustrations by Margaret Mayer
Cover photography by Steve Orlick
Child Management Logo by Steve Roe

Printed in the United States of America
10 9 8 7 6 5 4 3

For more information, contact:
Child Management, Inc.
800 Roosevelt Road
Glen Ellyn, Illinois 60137

Publisher's Cataloging in Publication
(Prepared by Quality Books Inc.)

Phelan, Thomas W., 1943-
    1-2-3 magic: effective discipline for children 2-12
Thomas W. Phelan. — 2nd ed.
    p. cm.
    ISBN 0-9633861-9-0

    1. Discipline of children,   I. Title. II. Title:
One-two-three magic.

HQ770.4.P44 1994   649'.64
                          QBI94-1214

To Eileen

Contents

PART III: NO CHILD WILL THANK YOU

PART IV: ENCOURAGING GOOD BEHAVIOR

PART V: THE 1-2-3 IN THE CLASSROOM

PART VI: YOUR CHILD'S SELF-ESTEEM

Preface to the
Second Edition

The very first *1-2-3 Magic* seminar took place at a local Holiday Inn on a cold April day in 1984. It was attended by twenty-eight parents.

That was 160,000 books, 43,000 videos and 725 seminars ago. Today the 1-2-3 method is rapidly becoming one of the most popular child-rearing programs in the country. We believe there are two reasons for this. It is very easy to learn. And it works.

The basic methods were developed over a period of years after the author got his doctorate, which was also about the time he became a father. Years and years of trial and error followed, in the role of both parent and therapist trying to help others manage youngsters.

This experimentation was not, of course, completely without guidance. Graduate school books and courses had taught some useful principles, such as positive reinforcement, active listening and operant conditioning. What had to be discovered from scratch, however, were the critical child-rearing principles that make *1-2-3 Magic* unique: the "little adult assumption," the distinction between "Start" and "Stop" behavior, the "No-Talking, No-Emotion" Rules, the six kinds of Testing and Manipulation, and the exact details of the counting procedure itself.

These essential pieces came from the seemingly interminable process of sending parents home with an assignment, having them come back and report how it worked, agreeing on modifications, trying out the new tactics, coming back, tuning it up again, and so on. Family after family after family. Although the process was at times tedious, it also involved the excitement of discovery and—at last!—the satisfaction of seeing the end result begin to work again and again and again.

From this crucible of collaboration, repeated experimentation and hard work came a product which will stand the test of time.

We owe a debt of gratitude to those parents whose struggles helped develop *1-2-3 Magic* in the years before 1984. And let's not forget their children, who served as our first "experimental subjects."

Also critical to the method's development was the cooperation and patience of my wife, Eileen, and, of course, the fun and the challenges presented to us at home by our children, Tom and Julie.

Had too few patients come through the office, the 1-2-3 might never have materialized. But two long-time friends and pediatricians, Roy Betti and Ron Eriksen, long ago saw to it that we wouldn't lack for work. Collaborating with them over the years in a spirit of openmindedness and cooperation has been invaluable.

Before the age of computers the original 1-2-3 book had to be typed by hand. This job was accomplished with skill and precision by Nancy Roe, who has also provided skillful assistance with the horrible task of proofreading. The painstaking effort and editorial expertise of B.J. Markel and Noah Liberman were also invaluable and very much appreciated.

The present version of the 1-2-3 has also been refined during hundreds and hundreds of workshops, which were set up by Peggy Farrell. Her organizational skills and conscientiousness have ensured that they run smoothly. The energy and expertise of Jana Larkin have been extremely helpful in both designing and marketing the *1-2-3 Magic* books.

Four new chapters for teachers, covering preschool to junior high children, were added to the second edition. Based on the actual experiences of school personnel, these additions have proven to be very helpful to those who wish to use the 1-2-3 in school settings. Thanks here go to Debbie Cook, Jan Cernock, Helen Callahan, Chuck Swangren, Paula

Rancilio, Susan Lawson, Frances Wilson, Tricia Goodell, Theresa Ouderkirk and Claire Taylor. With their help, these new chapters are down-to-earth and practical.

Applications of the 1-2-3 in community mental health centers have also added a lot to our knowledge of the usefulness of the program. Our thanks especially to the DuPage County Mental Health Center (Illinois), which for years has taught an expanded eight-session version of *1-2-3 Magic* called "Parents in Charge." In Canada, Team Leader Sig Taylor of the Young Children's Development Program of the Southeastern Alberta Health Unit has found a way to use the 1-2-3 to dramatically reduce intake overload and waiting lists for child evaluations.

Finally, thanks are due to Andy Olcott of Booklet Publishing Company for his advice, hard work and helpful suggestions over the years.

Due to the combined efforts of all these people, the *1-2-3 Magic* dream has become a reality.

How to Use This Book

The book that follows describes some very effective methods for managing the behavior of children from the ages of approximately two to twelve. To get the best results, keep in mind the following:

1. The methods must be used exactly as they are described here, especially with regard to the No-Talking and No-Emotion Rules.

2. If both parents are living at home, they should both use the techniques.

3. Single parents can use the methods effectively by themselves.

4. Grandparents, babysitters and other caregivers have also found the 1-2-3 very helpful in managing young children. In fact, many grandparents have first discovered *1-2-3 Magic* on their own and then shared it with their children.

5. The kids should be in good physical health.

Psychological counseling is indicated *before* using the methods in this book if any child has a history of excessive separation anxiety, physical violence or extremely self-punitive behavior. These children can be exceptionally difficult to manage during the initial testing period when they are still adjusting to the new discipline. If a family is currently in counseling, this book should be discussed with the counselor before being used.

Psychological evaluation and counseling are indicated *after* using the procedures described here if:

1. Marital instability or conflict are interfering with the effective use of the methods.

2. One or both parents are incapable of following the No-Talking and No-Emotion Rules.

3. Testing and Manipulation are continuing at a high level for more than three weeks.

Chapters 1-11 *must* be read before using the 1-2-3. It is preferable that they be read before using the methods in Chapters 12-28 as well.

In the second edition of *1-2-3 Magic*, a number of new chapters appeared. Along with the four chapters for teachers, new chapters included "What to Do in Public," "Active Listening," "Active Listening and Counting," and "10 Steps for Building Self-Esteem." Other chapters were extensively rewritten. The chapter on homework, for example, added lots of helpful ideas and new examples of using the 1-2-3 were provided.

We believe these changes made the second edition of *1-2-3 Magic* an even more valuable resource for parents, teachers and others who care for our children.

What's the Problem?

"**C**an I have a Twinkie?"

"No, dear."

"Why not?"

"'Cause we're eating at six o'clock."

"Yeah, but I want one."

"I just told you you couldn't have one."

"You never give me anything."

"What do you mean I never give you anything? Do you have clothes on? Is there a roof over your head? Am I feeding you in two seconds?!"

"You gave my brother one a half-hour ago."

"Listen, are you your brother? Besides, *he* eats his dinner."

"I promise I'll eat my dinner."

"Don't give me this promise, promise, promise stuff, Heather! Yesterday—4:30 in the afternoon—you had half a peanut butter and jelly sandwich and you didn't eat anything at dinner!"

"THEN I'M GOING TO KILL MYSELF AND THEN RUN AWAY FROM HOME!!"

Family Trouble

No one ever said parenting (or teaching) was easy. Living with young children can be one of life's most enjoyable experiences, but it can also become unbelievably frustrating if you don't quite know what you're doing.

There are those days when it seems half of the time the kids are doing what you *don't* want them to do, and the other half of the time they're not doing what you *do* want them to do.

Parents often forget that it is impossible to give kids everything they want. Raising and educating children means that, in addition to nurturing and supporting them, you must also frustrate them on a regular basis—for their own good and for the good of everyone. But when frustrated, kids have an amazing knack for sidetracking their parents or teachers, eliminating fun, destroying affection and—over the long run—ruining relationships.

Repeat the kitchen scene above a thousand times and you have guaranteed misery. That's no way for anyone to live and certainly no way for a child to grow up.

Children don't come with a training manual. Adults need to know how to handle difficult behavior, encourage good behavior, and manage the inevitable sidetrack of testing and manipulation—all in a manner that is fair, perfectly clear and not abusive. Although this may be a difficult task, it is critical to peaceful coexistence and to each child's ability to enjoy life and maintain healthy self-esteem.

Part I

Straight Thinking

1

Welcome to
the 1-2-3

1-2-3 *Magic* will teach you some very simple, precise and effective ways to manage your children in approximately the two-to-twelve-year-old age range. The methods that will be described are very easy to learn. You do not have to be a saint, genius or professional psychotherapist to use them properly. Too many parenting books simply tell you seventy-five mistakes you are making with your kids, then leave you feeling guilty with no clear place to take action.

When you finish with this book, you will know exactly what to do, what not to do, what to say, and what not to say in just about every one of the common, everyday problem situations you will run into with your kids. You will also know how to handle more serious difficulties. *You will find that, if you use the "1-2-3" correctly, it will work!* It has been shown to be very effective with two-to-twelve-year-olds, whether they are "problem" children or just typical youngsters. In fact, *1-2-3 Magic* has been used successfully with learning disabled, attention deficit and emotionally disturbed children, as well as with the visually and hearing impaired.

When you finish *1-2-3 Magic* (book, video or audio), it is a good idea to start the program immediately. Talk with your spouse, if both parents are living at home, and then get going right away. If you don't, you may never get around to it. If you are a single parent, take a deep breath and get started.

If you do start right away, things will change fast. There is good news and bad news here. The good news is that about half of the kids will fall into the "immediate cooperator" category. You can just relax and enjoy that. The bad news is that the other half will be "immediate testers." They are going to challenge you to see if you are serious and really mean business. If you stick to your guns, you can usually get this group shaped up pretty well in about a week to ten days.

Believe it or not, you might have a much more peaceful home, more enjoyable kids and better self-esteem—all in the foreseeable future!

Before we get into the details of the 1-2-3, we must clarify two very important concepts:

1. The two categories of problem behavior (Chapter 2).
2. The dangerous assumption parents (and teachers) make about children (Chapter 3).

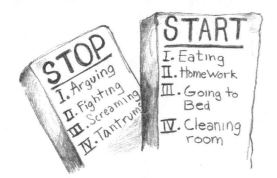

2

Start Behavior and Stop Behavior

When you are having problems with your kids, they are either 1) doing something you don't want them to do or that you want them to *stop*, or 2) they are not doing something you would like them to *start* doing. Therefore we call these two kinds of things "*Stop*" behavior and "*Start*" behavior.

Stop behaviors include the frequent, minor, everyday hassles kids get into, such as disrespect, temper tantrums, arguing, whining, fighting, pouting, yelling and so on. Each of these actions by itself may not be so bad, but add them all up in one afternoon and you may feel like hitchhiking to Seattle!

Start behaviors include things like cleaning rooms, homework, practicing obnoxious musical instruments, getting up and out in the morning, going to bed, eating, and the like. Here you want the child to do something that's good.

The reason for distinguishing between these two kinds of behaviors is this: you will use different tactics for each.

Here's how it works:

• For STOP BEHAVIOR such as...

    arguing
    fighting
    screaming
    tantrums
    teasing

you will use the 1-2-3 or "counting" proce-dure.

(Chapter 5)

• For START BEHAVIOR such as...

    eating
    doing homework
    going to bed
    cleaning rooms
    getting up and out in the morning

you will have a choice of six tactics (or combinations of them):

    1. Sloppy PVF
    2. Kitchen Timers
    3. The Docking System
    4. Natural Consequences
    5. Charting
    6. A variation of the 1-2-3
        (Chapter 14)

When managing a difficulty with one of your children, therefore, you will need to first determine if you have a Stop or a Start problem. If you mix up your tactics (e.g., use counting for homework), you will not get optimum results—or you may get no results at all.

You must also think realistically—and not wishfully—about your kids. You may have a dangerous false assumption floating around in your head regarding your children.

3

The Little Adult
Assumption

M any parents and teachers have an idea about kids that causes a lot of trouble. This false assumption leads either to discipline attempts that don't work or to stormy scenes that make everyone feel bad. This erroneous idea is known as the "little adult assumption."

The little adult assumption is the belief that kids have hearts of gold and are basically reasonable and unselfish—that they're just smaller versions of us. Thus, if your child is not doing his homework, you simply sit him down and explain to him the three golden, irrefutable reasons why he should: First, he will learn more. Second, it will make you and his teacher happy. And third, he will grow up to be a responsible and successful person. After receiving this wealth of wisdom, the child naturally responds by saying, "Gee, I never looked at it like that before," and immediately goes to his room to complete his work.

Or imagine your eight-year-old son is torturing his little sister for the fortieth time since they got home from school. You ask him how he would feel if someone did that to him. He says, "You know, you're right, I wouldn't like it very much. How insensitive I've been," and he stops—permanently.

How nice, but it just doesn't happen in real life. Kids are not little adults. Parents and teachers who believe—or want to believe—this myth are going to rely heavily on *words and reasons* in dealing with the kids and trying to change their behavior. And words and reasons are going to be miserable failures too much of the time. Sometimes they will have absolutely no impact at all. Other times they will take the parent and child through the *Talk-Persuade-Argue-Yell-Hit Syndrome.*

What is that, exactly? Your child is doing something you don't like. You try telling her why she shouldn't do it. She doesn't respond, so you start trying to persuade her to see things your way. When persuasion fails, you start arguing. Arguing leads to a yelling match, and when that fails, you may feel there is nothing left to do but hit. Actually, 90 per cent of spankings and the like are simply parental temper tantrums.

We're not implying here that you in particular are going around hitting your kids all the time. It may be true, however, that one of the main causes of child abuse (physical, not sexual) in this country is the little adult assumption. A parent reads in a book that talking is the preferred method. Then, when talking and reasoning fail, the parent goes crazy and starts hitting, because his favorite strategy isn't working, he is extremely frustrated and doesn't know what else to do.

Kids are kids—not little adults. A writer once said "Childhood is a period of transitory psychosis." She meant that kids, when they are little, are sort of nuts! They are born unreasonable and selfish, and it is our job—and a teacher's job—to help them become the opposite.

How do you do that? You start by changing your thinking about children. It may sound a little strange at first, but instead of thinking of your kids as little adults, think of yourself as a *wild animal trainer*! We don't mean, of course, using whips, guns or chairs. A wild animal trainer chooses a method—which is largely nonverbal—and repeats it until the "trainee" does what the trainer wants. The trainer is patient and gentle, but also persistent. Our job in *1-2-3 Magic* is to present some useful training methods to you, so that you can repeat them until the trainees, your children, do what you want them to. Fortunately, you do not usually have to repeat these things for ever and ever.

Dictatorship to Democracy

For those who are a little uncomfortable with this philosophy, thinking that it may be a little too heavy-handed, the overall orientation of *1-2-3 Magic* is what you might call "dictatorship to democracy." When your kids are little, your house should be a dictatorship where you are the judge and jury. When the kids are in their mid to late teens, your house should be more of a democracy, where the youngsters have more to say about the rules and policies that affect them. Even then, though, when push comes to shove, who's paying the mortgage? You are. And who knows better than they do what's good for them? You do. And you have a right—and duty—to impose limits on them, even if they don't like it.

What if you have children who do respond to words and reasons? You are certainly lucky! Recent research has indicated that there are three such children in the United States. If you have one or more of them, you may not need this book. Or, if they ever stop responding to logic, you can consider using the 1-2-3.

4

The Two
Biggest Mistakes

The two biggest mistakes that parents and teachers make in dealing with children are: Too Much Talking and Too Much Emotion. Talking is bad because it either doesn't work or it takes you through the *Talk-Persuade-Argue-Yell-Hit Syndrome.*

Why is too much emotion destructive? When they are little, kids feel inferior. They feel inferior because they *are* inferior. Sure, they can be cute and lovable and nice, but they are also smaller, less privileged, less intelligent, less skillful, less responsible and less of just about everything than their parents and the older kids. And this "lessness" bugs them a lot! They don't like it. They do like to feel they are powerful and capable of making some mark on the world.

Have you ever seen a small child go down to a lake and throw rocks in the water? Children can do that for hours, partly because the big splashes are a sign of their impact. They are making that happen.

What does rock tossing have to do with what happens at home? Simple. If this small child can get big old you all upset, your upset is the big splash for him. It's not that he has no conscience and is going to grow up to be a criminal. It's just that having all that power temporarily

15

rewards—or feels good to—the inferior part of the child. Parents who say, "It drives me absolutely crazy when she eats her dinner with her fingers. Why does she do that?" may have already answered their own question. She may do that at least partly *because it drives them crazy.*

An important corollary: *if you have a child who is doing something you don't like, get real upset about it on a regular basis and, sure enough, she'll repeat it for you.*

There are certainly discipline systems other than the 1-2-3, but you will certainly ruin any of them by talking too much and getting too excited. These two mistakes, of course, usually go hand in hand, and the emotion involved is usually anger.

Some parents can turn off the talking and the emotional upset like a faucet, and others have to work like dogs to get the job done. Even then, they often have to remind themselves over and over that talking and arguing and yelling and screaming don't really help. These tactics merely blow off steam for a few seconds. If parents find that they can't shake these habits, some sort of outpatient counseling or psychotherapy is indicated.

Part II

Controlling Obnoxious Behavior

5

The 1-2-3

So, if the wild animal trainer model does not allow too much talking and too much emotion, how exactly does it work? The procedure we'll discuss here will be the 1-2-3. Before we describe how it works, there are two things that must be pointed out.

First, you will use the 1-2-3, or counting method, to deal with Stop behaviors. In other words, you will be counting things like arguing, fighting, whining, yelling, tantrums, etc. You will not use it to get the child to get up in the morning or practice the violin.

Second, after you hear how to do the 1-2-3, you are likely to be skeptical. It may seem too easy. You may think, "Hey, buddy, you don't know my kid—this kid is a wild man!" Don't worry about feeling this way; the 1-2-3 is deceptively simple, but it is not always easy. It is very powerful *provided that you follow the No-Talking and No-Emotion Rules.* Many parents, though, finish the book or video and feel doubtful. After a few days, however, they say, "I can't believe it—it works like magic!"

There is no magic in *1-2-3 Magic*. It simply represents the careful, logical and persistent extension of certain common-sense ideas and behavioral principles in the discipline and training of children.

Undoubtedly, after the initial explanation, you will have questions. We will attempt to answer all of your questions in a few chapters, and then you can begin.

How does the 1-2-3 work? Imagine you have a four-year-old child (which many of you do). He is having a major temper tantrum on the kitchen floor at 6 p.m. because you wouldn't give him any potato chips right before dinner. He is banging his head on the floor, kicking the cabinets for all he's worth, and screaming bloody murder. You are at a loss for what to do.

You recall that your pediatrician told you to ignore it. Your mother told you to put a cold washcloth over the kid's face. And your husband told you to beat the daylights out of him!

None of these are acceptable alternatives. With the 1-2-3, you hold up one finger, look down at the little devil, and say, "That's 1."

He doesn't care. He's insane with rage and keeps his tantrum going full force. So you let a few seconds go by, then hold up two fingers and say, "That's 2." Same reaction. So after a few more seconds, you hold up three fingers and say, "That's 3, take 5." This means that he has had two chances to shape up and he blew it—he didn't shape up. So he goes off to his room for a "rest period" or "time out." (Some of you are wondering, "How do I get him there?!" We'll talk about that later.)

The child serves the time out. (By the way, a good rule of thumb for the length of the time out is one minute for each year of the child's age; a five-year-old gets five minutes, a ten-year-old gets ten, etc.) When the child comes out from the rest period, nothing at all is said about what happened, unless absolutely necessary.

You do not say, for example, "Now, are you going to be a good boy? Why do we have to go through this every day? I've told you a thousand times that you can't eat right before dinner, but you never seem to listen to me. Now you know your sister doesn't behave that way, and your father's going to be home any minute now, so you don't want to...blah, blah, blah..."

You simply remain quiet. If the child does something else that's countable, feel free to count it. After a while, you'll get good control—believe it or not—at 1 or 2. Some kids will always take you to 2, prompting some parents to wonder, "Don't you think he's manipulating us, always taking it to 2?" The answer is, "No, he's not manipulating you always taking you to 2." What really drives people crazy is 42, or 72, or a child who has to be told a thousand times before he'll shape up. Two times is not bad at all, and if the child hits 3, he's gone.

Other parents ask, with good reason, "What if the kid does something that's so bad, you don't want him to have three chances to do it?" For example, what if your child hits you? Your kids can't hit you. If your child does hit you, it would be ludicrous to say, "That's 1," and give him two more shots. So if the behavior is bad enough to begin with, you simply say, "That's three, take 5 and add 15 more for the seriousness of the offense."

What if your child called you a bad name he had just learned on the playground? Same thing. "That's 3, take 5, and add 15 more for the rotten mouth." And when that youngster returns from time out, an explanation would be in order concerning what the word meant and why he can't use it in your house.

The No-Talking and No-Emotion Rules

Occasionally, people say something like, "Hey, we've used this counting stuff and it just doesn't work for us. Counting is just no good." Ninety-plus percent of the time the problem here is easy to spot: the people are not really using the 1-2-3 properly. Here's how the scene might go if they were back trying to manage our four-year-old temper tantrum artist:

> "That's 1. Come on now, I'm getting a little sick and tired
> of this. I don't know why you can't do just one little thing for
> me—LOOK AT ME WHEN I'M TALKING TO YOU!—
> when we're always doing everything for you."
> "OK, that's 2! One more and you're history, young man. Do
> you really enjoy going to your room or do you just get a kick
> out of trying to drive me crazy?!" (Pause for breath)
> "OK, I'VE HAD IT! THAT'S 3! GET OUT OF MY SIGHT!
> I NEVER WANT TO SEE YOU AGAIN! EVER! TAKE FIVE!
> BEAT IT!"

Who's Responsible?

That's not the 1-2-3. It is, however, a major violation of our two cardinal rules: No Talking and No Emotion. An interesting thing happens when you go on and on like that. When you start out with "That's 1" and then stop talking, the ball's in the child's court. He's responsible by himself for changing his behavior. But if you keep talking, a strange thing happens. You take over that responsibility, and the whole discipline scene changes. The rule now is he doesn't have to shape up *unless you can produce three or four good (acceptable to him) reasons* why he should. And it will be a long, long time before the average frustrated child in this situation mellows out—because of your words—sees the light and says, "Gee, I never looked at it like that before!"

Other problems occur if parents violate our two cardinal rules. One is that the child can't clearly hear or pick out the warning ("That's 1") when it's mixed up with all the rest of that verbal garbage. If you have a child with Attention Deficit Disorder who doesn't pay attention very well in the first place, his attending only to the warning itself is even less likely.

Another problem is that when you yell and nag and argue at youngsters, many of them will take it as a challenge and you will have a war on your hands. There are plenty of kids who would sooner cut off their left leg than lose a good fight. Unwise attempts at talking or persuading *are guaranteed to take the child's focus off the possibility of good behavior and put the focus on the possibility of an enjoyable argument.*

So if the child is acting up, it's "That's 1 [button your lip]," "That's 2 [quiet]," and so on.

Sometimes your silence can speak louder than your words.

The Famous Twinkie Example

Our famous Twinkie example will help you better understand the workings of the 1-2-3. Here is a situation most of you parents have experienced in one way or another. You are cooking dinner at 5:45 p.m. and your eight-year-old daughter walks into the kitchen:

"Can I have a Twinkie?"

"No, dear."

"Why not?"

"Because we're eating at six o'clock."

So far, so good, right? This has been a perfectly reasonable conversation to this point; the child asks a clear question and the parent gives a clear answer. The problem is that most kids are not going to leave it there; they're going to press further by adding, in a whiny voice, "Yeah, but I want one."

So what are you going to do?

Let's play out this situation three ways. In Scene I, Mom believes in the little adult assumption: words and reasons will change this kid's behavior. We'll see what happens with that approach.

In Scene II, the mother will be wising up. She will be starting to use the 1-2-3, but the child won't be used to it yet.

In Scene III, the mother will still be using the 1-2-3, and the little girl will have grown more accustomed to it.

Scene I: starring the mother who believes in words and reason:

"Can I have a Twinkie?"

"No, dear."

"Why not?"

"'Cause we're eating at six o'clock."

"Yeah, but I want one."

"I just told you you couldn't have one."

"You never give me anything."

"What do you mean I never give you anything? Do you have
   clothes on? Is there a roof over your head? Am I feeding
   you in two seconds?!"

"You gave my brother one a half-hour ago."

"Listen, are you your brother? And besides, *he* eats his
   dinner."

"I promise I'll eat my dinner."

"Don't give me this promise, promise, promise stuff, Heather!
   Yesterday—4:30 in the afternoon—you had half a peanut
   butter and jelly sandwich and you didn't eat anything at dinner!"

"THEN I'M GOING TO KILL MYSELF AND THEN
  RUN AWAY FROM HOME!!"
"WELL, BE MY GUEST. I'M SICK OF THIS!!"

You can see where trying to talk at the wrong time will get you.

In the next scene, Mom gets smart and starts using the 1-2-3, but it's new and the child is still getting used to it.

Scene II: starring the mother beginning to use the 1-2-3:

"Can I have a Twinkie?"
"No, dear."
"Why not?"
"Because we're eating at six o'clock."
"Yeah, but I want one."
"That's 1."
"You never give me anything!"
"That's 2."
"THEN I'M GOING TO KILL MYSELF AND THEN
  RUN AWAY FROM HOME!!"
"That's 3, take 5."

Mom did well. The child disappears for a rest period and the episode is over.

How's it going to go when the child is more used to counting and is realizing that testing and manipulation are useless?

Scene III: the 1-2-3 after a few days:

"Can I have a Twinkie?"
"No, dear."
"Why not?"
"Because we're eating at six o'clock."
"Yeah, but I want one."
"That's 1."
(Pause) "Oh, all right." (Grumpy exit from kitchen)

Good work by Mom. She doesn't have to count the grumpy "Oh, all right" because it's not so bad and the child is leaving. If the child said, "Oh, all right, stupid jerk!" there would be an automatic 3 and off to the room.

What's Good About the 1-2-3?

The 1-2-3 will save you a lot of breath—and a lot of aggravation. Parents and teachers say it makes discipline a whole lot less exhausting. One explanation—if absolutely necessary, and then you count. There is no extra talking and no extra emotion. You stay calmer and you feel better when you get a good response at 1 or 2.

Also, your authority with the 1-2-3 is not negotiable. It shouldn't be. You are the boss, and, as a matter of fact, you as the parent must frustrate your kids on a regular basis because you can't possibly give them everything they want. Many parents, though, complicate the job of discipline by setting for themselves two goals instead of just one. The first goal is to discipline the children, which is fine. But the second goal is *to get the kids to like it!* Like the mother in Scene I, the parent talks and talks and talks, waiting for the youngster to say something like, "Gee, I never looked at it like that before. Thanks for taking the time to explain it to me. I appreciate your efforts to raise me to be a responsible child." Then the child happily gives up the battle.

That doesn't usually happen. If the child does listen and the talking seems to help, fine. But with a frustrated child that is not usually the case, and too often the talking graduates to arguing.

One more reason the 1-2-3 works so well is that the punishment is short and sweet: about one minute per year of the child's life. The brief consequence does not make the child so mad that when he comes out he wants war. With this regimen, most kids come back from time out and just forget about it. And remember, you are not allowed to bring up what happened unless it is absolutely necessary.

When is an explanation or more talking absolutely necessary? In those instances when the problem involved is something that the child definitely does not already understand, when what he did is something that is unusual and fairly serious, or when you really need more information from him about what happened.

Here's an example. Your seven-year-old son has been learning trampoline in gym class. After school he comes home, takes off his shoes, and starts jumping up and down on the couch in the family room. You say, "That's 1," and he says, "What did I do?" An explanation is in order. You tell him that although he took off his shoes, you're afraid he'll hurt himself or ruin the couch.

When is an explanation not necessary? A few hours later, the same seven-year-old—for no apparent reason—gives his younger sister a shove right in front of you. You say, "That's 1" and he growls, "WHAT DID I DO?!" You say, "That's 2." Stupid question.

The 1-2-3 is also easy enough to learn that you can train babysitters, grandparents and other caretakers to use it. Then the kids get the same message from everyone.

To some people the 1-2-3 can appear almost too simple. It *is* very straightforward, but raising kids is never an easy job. In fact, at this point your mind is probably filled with quite a few questions. Let's take a look at some of the important ones that have come up most frequently over the years.

6

Frequently Asked Questions

How long do you take in between counts?

Just long enough to allow the child time to shape up, or about 3 to 5 seconds. You're not going to give the child half an hour to continue the tantrum before you hit him with the 2. Nor would you say "That's 1" at nine in the morning, "That's 2" at eleven, and "That's 3, take 5" at three in the afternoon. Kids' time perspective reaches about five minutes forward and five back. So we have what we call our *20 (or 30) Minute Rule:* if the child does three things wrong in any twenty-minute period, each one counts toward the total of three. But if he does one thing, twenty minutes or more pass, and then he does something else, you start back at one. Very few children will get manipulative with this, doing one thing, allowing twenty minutes to pass, and then figuring, "Now I get a free one!"

Note: many teachers do not use the 20 Minute Rule because, with 25 children in your class, this potentially allows for too much misbehavior in too short a period of time. Instead, the rule is expanded to cover a whole class period or even half of the day, depending on the ages of the kids.

Does the 1-2-3 cause the child to hate his room?

Not if you do it right. If the 1-2-3 is done correctly, it is simple and matter-of-fact. What may cause a child to hate his room, however, is all the yelling, name-calling, belittling, sarcasm or hitting you may do if you don't use this method.

Does the room have to be a sterile environment?

No. Many books tell you the time-out room should be modeled after a cell in a state penitentiary. This is unnecessary. The child can go to the room and read, take a nap, listen to the radio, play with Legos, and so on. She doesn't even have to stay on her bed. Just to be safe, though, there are three things that are forbidden: no phone, no friends along, and no TV, Nintendo or computer games.

Some people ask: "Well then, how does the 1-2-3 work? My kid just tells me that time out's fine with her—she doesn't care and she'll just go upstairs and play." Don't pay much attention to any child who says, "I don't care." That comment usually means she does care. And if her room were such a great place to be, she would have already been up there. The fact of the matter is, the power of the 1-2-3 does not come so much from the time out itself; it comes from the interruption of the child's activities. No one—including you—likes to be interrupted.

Can you count different things to get to three?

Yes. In fact, you have to. It would drive you crazy if you had to begin new counts for each type of misbehavior. So if the child pushes his sister, "That's 1," throws a block across the room, "That's 2," and then (within 20 minutes) screams at you, "That's 3, take 5," and the child is gone.

Mom could say 1, Dad could say 2, and Mom or Dad could say, "That's 3." In fact, we encourage you to share the joy and spread it around some. Actually, it's better if Mom and Dad *do* do this, because then the kids know that both parents are behind the program and are really serious. The involvement of both parents makes it easier for the children to shape up.

Can you ever ignore anything?

Yes, but don't in the beginning. *In the beginning, when in doubt, count!* After a while, when you're getting a good response at 1 or 2, you may be able to let up a little. Let's say, after getting used to the program, your child does something right in front of you that would normally be counted. Now the child can almost "feel" the count coming. Sometimes, if you say nothing, the child will spontaneously self-control and stop the misbehavior. This response is ideal, because now the child is internalizing the rules.

How do you know when you should count? It's not too difficult to tell. Most of the time, if you're irritated about something and that something is a Stop behavior, you should be counting. Just to be sure, you can also write yourself a list (or do it with your spouse) of countable behaviors and then show it to the kids. Some parents and teachers even have the children help make up the list.

What if you have other people over?

For our purposes here, the other people who come over fall into three categories: other kids, other parents (with or without their kids), and, finally, grandparents.

Other kids. If your youngster has a friend over, count just as you would if no one else were there. If your child gets timed out, he goes to the room and—remember—his friend may not join him. Just explain to the other kid that you're using this weird system and his buddy will be back in five minutes or so. If your son or daughter says to you, as some have, "Dad, it's so embarrassing when you count me in front of my friends," you say to them once, "If you don't want to be embarrassed, you can behave."

Another thing you can do in this situation is count the other child, too. After all, it's your house. If his parent is there, though, you'd better ask permission before you go disciplining her child.

Another variation, especially if you have a difficult child, is "1-2-3, 1-2-3, 1-2-3: out of the house to play." That means that at the third time out, instead of sending your child to the room again, both kids must now leave the house for a specified time (assuming the weather isn't brutal). Or—even better—1-2-3, 1-2-3, 1-2-3, then send them over to the other kid's house to play for a while!

Other adults. If you have other people over to your house, get used to counting your child in front of them. You may feel a little self-conscious at first, but it's a good idea to get used to doing the 1-2-3 under these circumstances. Otherwise, your children will sense that you are much easier prey when other parents are around.

When you count in front of another parent, something surprising may happen. You say, "That's 1," and your child stops goofing around. The other parent may look at you like, "What did you do?!" Just tell that parent about the 1-2-3 and explain how it works.

Grandparents. With regard to the 1-2-3, there are three types of grandparents, whether you're visiting them or they're visiting you. The first—and rarest—type of grandparent is the *cooperative* grandparent. She will count along with you. You say 1, Grandma says 2, and so on. But that doesn't happen a lot.

The second type of grandparent is also nice to have around: the *passive* grandparent. She doesn't get involved, but she leaves you alone and doesn't interfere either. That's fine.

The third type of grandparent is the *antagonistic* grandparent. She will say something to you like, "You had to read a book to learn how to raise your kids?! Why, when I was a girl, all daddy had to do was look at his belt...," and so on. Her message is that you don't need any of this modern, psychological stuff.

Another kind of antagonistic grandparent will get in your way. You say to little Bobby, "That's 3, take 5," and before he moves Grandma butts in and says, "Oh, little Bobby didn't really do anything. Bobby, come and sit on Grandma's lap for a while."

Some parents ask at this point: "Can you count the grandparents?" Probably not, but you do have an assertiveness problem on your hands. You may have to say something like, "You know, Mom, I love you very much, but these are our kids and this is the way we're raising them. If you can't go along with the agenda, the visit may have to be cut short a little." Not easy to do, but important.

Can you imagine saying that to your parents?!

Can you use a time-out chair instead of the room?

You can use a time-out stair or chair, but only if the child does not goof around on it. Some kids, for example, sit on the chair at first, but eventually move totally off. Then they just touch their little finger to the chair and look at you like, "What are you going to do about this?" This kind of game will ruin the discipline.

We usually prefer that visual contact between parent and child be broken during the rest period, so the child can't play games or provoke. Some parents, however, have already been successfully using chairs and many report that the kids sit still on them, don't talk too much, and don't keep getting off. That's fine.

There is also nothing sacred about the youngster's bedroom. Alternate rooms can be used if they are more convenient, as long as they are safe.

What if the child won't go to his room?

If the child won't go to his room after you hit a count of three, remember that you are not allowed to use little adult attempts at persuasion, such as, "Come on now, do what Dad told you. It's only for five minutes and then you'll be able to go back and play—why can't you just do this one little thing for me?...etc., etc."

What you do instead depends on how big you are and how big the child is. Let's say you are 125 pounds, and your five-year-old son weighs 45. If he doesn't go to his room at 3, you simply move toward him. Some kids will then stay two feet ahead of you all the way to the room. That's OK. Others have to be "escorted" (keep your mouth shut while doing this), which can mean gently taking them by the arm, as well as dragging or carrying them. That is, if you're 125 pounds and they're 45.

Now let's imagine that it's five years later. Your 10-year-old now weighs 95 pounds, and you—through a rigid program of diet and exercise—still weigh 125. You are no longer in a position to get into anything physical with this kid. He's too big, and wrestling matches make a fool out of you and any attempts at discipline. What you do instead is say, "That's 3, take 10, or it's a 50-cent fine (or some other minor consequence). You pick."

The youngster has a choice: a rest period or a fine. If he says, "Neither!", then it's the fine, because you're in no position to wrestle him to his room. You say that 50 cents doesn't mean anything to a ten-year-old these days? You might be right. Then double the fine, triple it, or convert it into lost TV minutes.

A problem emerges here, though, because the child hasn't gone to the room and isn't out of sight. Lots of kids in this situation are going to want to stick around and argue with you about your stupid rules. But you're not allowed to argue. Instead, you pull a "reverse time out," in which *you* exit the premises. Go to your room or the bathroom, stock them with good reading materials, and wait the storm out. Or walk around the house a few times. But don't talk.

What if the child won't stay in his room?

Many kids will stay in the room just fine, even if the door isn't shut (it doesn't have to be). Others, however, will keep coming out. One alternative is to just stand there or hold the door shut, but this won't work if you keep getting into major tugs of war on the door knob. Once again, if your discipline comes down to this, you look stupid and so do your methods.

Another alternative is to add minutes to the time out (or double it) if the child comes out prematurely. This, of course, won't be much help with two- or three-year-olds because they won't understand, but with older children it can work well. Explain once and then start.

Some kids, however, are so rambunctious that they will just keep coming out and accumulate a million or so extra time-out minutes. So what should you do? Put a lock on the door. This advice worries some parents, who think that their child will become claustrophobic or that locking the door is abusive.

What you do is tell the child that as long as he stays in the room, the door can remain open or unlocked. But the first time he comes out, the door gets locked for the rest period. Many children will quickly learn to stay put without the door having to be locked.

Many others, though, including some of our Attention Deficit (ADD) friends, will keep coming out no matter what you do, and locking them in is necessary. It is totally unproductive and harmful to have to be chasing them back in the room all the time, so the child must know that the door is a barrier that he's stuck with until the time is up. If you worry about the safety of the child, childproof the room and remain outside the door during the time out, but don't let the child know you're there. And remember the one-minute-per-year rule for the duration of the rest period.

What if the child won't come out?

You probably know the answer to this one: relax and enjoy yourself! Try not to cheat on extending the time out, though. Keep an eye on the clock or timer, then when the time is up tell the child and unlock the door (if necessary). If when you unlock the door, the youngster says, "I'm never coming out again as long as I live!" don't take the bait. Just walk away.

Some kids always want a hug and some reassurance when time out is over. What do you do? Give them a hug! But be careful with these little huggers. If a child repeatedly requests a hug, you'd better check to make sure you're doing the 1-2-3 correctly. Does the child need this kind of reassurance because you were too harsh—emotionally or physically—before you sent him to the room?

How do you handle the Horrors of the Telephone?

This question brings back vivid memories to all parents. It seems that there are no parents in the entire world whose children don't act up when the parents are on the phone. Lots of kids start running around and screaming as soon as the thing rings, and they are often joined by the family pets!

What you do is count the children just as you would if you weren't on the phone. It's much like the earlier question about doing the 1-2-3 when you have other people over. You may have to interrupt the conversation to count. You may have to put the phone down or hang up before escorting a kid to her room. Long distance calls can become more expensive, but whatever it takes, do it. Otherwise the children will know that you are a sitting duck every time someone calls.

On a brighter note, some families get so good at doing the 1-2-3 that they don't say anything when counting. They simply hold up the appropriate number of fingers and the children respond. If you have gotten to this point, it's a handy tactic to use when you're talking on the telephone.

Does it hurt the child's self-esteem, being counted all the time?

Many kids aren't counted very much, so that's no problem. For those who do get counted more often, if you are doing the 1-2-3 correctly, there should be no problem with hurting self-esteem. The answer here reminds us of the earlier question about kids hating their rooms: what *will* hurt their self-esteem is all the yelling, arguing, name-calling, belittling, sarcasm or hitting you may do if you don't use this program. In addition, as you will see later, you can also balance off the counting (which is a kind of criticism) with "Sloppy PVF" (Positive Verbal Feedback).

What if the kid wrecks the room during his so-called "rest period"?

By far, the vast majority of children will not be room wreckers. This question is included, however, for two reasons. First of all, a small percentage of kids will kick holes in the wall, break things, and otherwise mess up the room, and their parents will need to know how to handle these actions. Second, the whole point behind *1-2-3 Magic* is that parents be ready for anything, rather than being defensive and thinking, "Oh no, what is he going to do now?"

We want your attitude and message to the children to be something like, "You're my child and I'm your parent. I love you, and it's my job to train and discipline you. I don't expect you to be perfect, and when you do do something wrong, here's what I'll do."

The credit for the solution to the room-wrecking problem comes from a couple who visited my office a long time ago. They had an eight-year-old boy who was very nice in the office, but "hell on wheels" everywhere else.

This behavior couldn't go on, so Mom and Dad learned the 1-2-3 and went home to get started. This boy had been used to running the house. In fact, his parents kiddingly said they were thinking of putting his name on the mailbox! However, they were ready for him when they went home.

When the boy hit 3 for the first time, he couldn't believe it. How his parents got him to his room is still a mystery, but when he got there, he trashed the place. His first tactic—and perhaps the favorite of all room-wreckers—was to empty his dresser and distribute his clothes all over the floor. Then he took the blankets and sheets off his bed and threw them around. Then the mattress and box springs were pushed off the bed frame. Next, he proceeded to his closet, took out all his hanging clothes, and threw them all over the room. Finally, he tore down his curtains.

What did his parents do? First of all, they didn't clean up the mess or have him clean it up. That would only have been loading his gun for the next time out: a perfectly neat room to wreck again. Second, they continued to count him aggressively. They didn't wimp out when he had a 2, and do fractions like, "That's 2.5, that's 2.7, that's 2.9," etc. They just hit him with the 3 and then sent him to the room to rearrange the trash. When bedtime came, he had to find his pajamas. He also had to find his bed. In the mornings, his clothes for school didn't match for a week.

It took about 10 days for him to calm down. Then, after three or four days of peaceful time outs, his parents helped him clean up his room. After that —believe it or not—he hated to be counted, and behaved very well at home and at school, where the teacher was also using the 1-2-3. Now he was the nice kid who had been seen in the office, and his parents were in charge at home as they should have been.

Two other things are important if you think you are going to have a room-wrecker. If there is anything dangerous or harmful in the room, or anything valuable that can be broken, take it out before the first "rest period." For example, if the child has a hammer and a saw in the room, or if Grandma has her Hummel collection on top of his dresser, get those out of there before you start counting.

What if the kids count you back or count each other?

It doesn't count, so to speak. You're the only one who has the authority to do the 1-2-3. If they are just teasing you when they count you back, ignore it. If they are really being nasty, count it.

Can't you ever talk to your kids?

When reading *1-2-3 Magic*, a few people have gotten the impression that you're never supposed to talk to your children. This certainly isn't the case. The main idea is that you don't discuss things with a kid *when a rule is being enforced*. That just encourages testing. The rest of the time, however, you can talk your head off if you want to. In fact, after the 1-2-3 has been used for a while, there will be a lot more time free for pleasant conversations. There will also be a lot more time for affection and fun, since less time is wasted in useless arguing or yelling.

Think of it like this: *discuss problems, but count attacks*. If a child wants to talk something over with you, that's fine (see Chapter 26, Active Listening). It's also OK—up to a point—if the child's frustrated and angry and is expressing those feelings. But if his presentation degenerates into simply repeating himself over and over, or into temper and verbal attacks on you, it should get counted (see Chapter 10, The Six Kinds of Testing and Manipulation).

Shouldn't the kids ever apologize?

If you're currently asking the kids to apologize, and that's working well, fine. Keep in mind, however, that many apologies are really exercises in hypocrisy. A forced and quite begrudging "I'm sorry" from a child's mouth may embarrass him, but it may also be asking him to lie.

Should you ever spank a child?

There may be a time when a "spanking" is appropriate. For example, as you escort a child to his room, he physically attacks you—kicking, hitting, scratching or biting. If a simple smack on the rear end (not full force and not repeated) helps him cooperate, fine.

However, one gruesome fact remains: *99 per cent of all spankings are parental temper tantrums*. They are in no way attempts to train. They are simply the angry outburst of a parent who has lost control, doesn't know what to do, and who wants to inflict pain. Most parents who want to justify spanking kids are parents who have big problems with anger management. Remember, the whole point of the 1-2-3 program is to avoid the Talk-Persuade-Argue-Yell-Hit routine.

Have we taken care of all possible questions? Not quite. The most commonly asked question needs a whole chapter devoted to it: *what do you do in public?*

7

What to Do in Public

After they have learned how the 1-2-3 works, many parents worry about what to do in public. Often their first thought is that there is no time-out room. Don't worry. Believe it or not, that problem can be solved, and it won't be the biggest problem you'll run into in public—by a longshot!

Your biggest problem is that the little devils can hold something over your head in public that they can't in private: *the threat of public embarrassment!* No one wants to look like a child abuser in the candy section of their local grocery store. And kids can sense this vulnerability well before they are two years old.

So what are you going to do? The first thing you have to accept is that you will probably get burned in public more than in private. Studies of parents of hyperactive or ADD kids, for example, consistently show that these parents report they have their worst times when out of the house. The same may very well be true for all kids, but that certainly does not mean you are helpless. You have several options which can help a lot.

1. Don't Take Them Unless You Have To

Have you ever been to church on Sunday, and in the row ahead of you there is a couple with a two-year-old? The two-year-old isn't paying any attention to the service, and neither are his parents, since they are so preoccupied with trying to keep him in line. Around this trio are 10 other people who aren't paying any attention to the service either, because they're busy evaluating how well the couple is disciplining their two-year-old.

So, in effect, we have 13 people who might as well have not gone to church at all. Of course, we're not trying to talk you out of going to church, but think before you go anywhere, and don't ask for unnecessary trouble.

2. The Basic 1-2-3

There are plenty of times, naturally, when you must go out and you must take the kids. So imagine now that you are in the candy aisle of the grocery store. Your five-year-old asks for a candy bar, you say No, and— BOOM!—the kid has a major temper tantrum right there on the floor, complete with kicking, head banging and yelling that can be heard out in the parking lot. What do you do?

You look down at the unhappy little monster, hold up one finger and say, "That's 1." You say it as calmly and as firmly as you would at home, trying your best not to be intimidated by the threat of public embarrassment and whispering, " Come on now, I don't want you making a fool of me in the candy section of the grocery store." You do that and the child will *know* that you can be had for a nickel; he won't need the candy bar because he's about to have you for lunch.

Proceed to 2 and then to 3, if necessary. Many parents now wonder, "What are we going to do at 3? There's no time-out room here." It's true there's no time-out room, but there are plenty of time-out *places*. Over the years, we've collected the ideas of many creative parents who, in the heat of battle, were forced to come up with someplace for the rest period.

Here are a few of their ideas:

1. The grocery cart (for small children)
2. The corner of the store

3. The store's bathroom
4. Right where you stand—holding their hand
5. The car for a few minutes
6. The front of the store. Send them there by themselves if they're old enough.

During the time out, you do not talk to the child. No lecturing, screaming or nagging. It's hard, but after a while the youngster gets the idea you mean business. And yes, there have been parents who felt the fuss was bad enough that they left a half-full grocery cart and went home.

3. The '1-2-3-4'

Here's another idea. It's 5:15 p.m. You're cooking a new recipe for dinner when you suddenly realize you are missing three essential ingredients. To make matters worse, your six-year-old and eight-year-old are in the other room playing well together for the first time in two and a half years, and you're going to have to interrupt them. There's no time to get a sitter.

Here's what you do. Tell the kids that you have to go shopping, it will take about an hour, and they have to go with you. You know they don't want to, but you're all stuck. But the deal is this: if they're "good" while you're out (meaning they don't hit a count of 3 or 4, depending on the length of the trip), you'll buy them a treat. Their reward might be 50 or 75 cents worth of candy or whatever, provided they don't get the final count.

Some parents feel this is bribery. It is! But the real definition of bribery is paying someone to do something illegal. Here we're paying the kids to do something legal, and it works.

One family used this method when taking the kids out for a treat (ice cream) in the first place. The first time they tried it, the kids started their usual fighting in the back seat. Dad said, "That's 1, third time ends the trip." (A count of 3 was used because it was a short ride.) The kids then hit 2, and then 3. Dad turned the car around and drove back home. Several days later, the same thing happened: no one got any ice cream.

The next time they tried the ice cream trip, the kids must have finally believed Dad was serious. They hit a count of one, and then were good as gold the rest of the way.

4. Keep Moving

Another tactic that some parents have used successfully takes us back to our grocery store example, with the youngster having a major fit in the candy section of aisle 5. What these parents have done is simply leave the child on the floor and move on to aisle 6. When they meet someone in aisle 6, they say, "Boy, do you hear all that racket over there?" Seriously, what often happens is that the child starts worrying where Mom or Dad went, forgets the candy, and runs to find them. Then again, some kids run to find their parent and then remember the candy and continue the tantrum. In that case you must return to the basic 1-2-3 mentioned above. If they *still* don't stop, you gut it out and finish your shopping, take them out to the car until they stop, or take them home.

Riding in the Car

Traveling in the car can present parents with some extremely difficult situations. Have you ever been riding along an interstate with your left hand on the wheel while your right hand is waving madly through the back seat trying to whack the kid who's just been teasing his sister for the 1,000th time since you left the last town? This is not fun, and it can ruin vacations.

Travelling in the car presents different problems for short trips and long trips. Here is what you can do:

Short trips

The basic 1-2-3 is very useful when chauffeuring the kids around town. The question is what to do at 3. One family didn't allow anyone to talk— including Mom and Dad—for fifteen minutes after the kids hit three. Other families have used fines (money taken off the allowance), usually at the rate of one or two cents for each minute that would have been included in the child's normal time out. A very effective tactic for many parents has been 1-2-3 and then pull the car off to the side of the road for the time out. It's rather dramatic and has quite an impact on the children.

Counting the kids in the car but having them serve the time outs when they get home isn't such a good idea, unless you're pretty close to home.

The problem is that the rest period comes too long after the offense to do much good. The demand for a time out simply starts a fight as soon as you get home, because often by then everybody has forgotten what happened.

Long trips

Long trips with small children can be especially horrendous experiences unless parents are ready and know what to do. One of the biggest problems is sibling rivalry and all the fighting that goes with it. The car becomes more like a prison on wheels. Mom and Dad are trapped.

One tactic that works well with small children is having the kids earn their spending money for the trip by not fighting. Why give them all that dough without getting something—like peace and quiet—in return? The deal is this: for every fifteen minutes the children go without fighting, they each earn 10 to 25 cents. *But there is a catch: either they both earn it, or they both lose it.* There is no time when one gets the reward and the other doesn't. Take some paper and a timer with you in the car to keep an accurate accounting.

Other tactics that parents have used successfully have included the usual—and very helpful—things like the alphabet game and car bingo. Putting one child in the front and one in the back has been useful, as has renting a VCR that plugs into the cigarette lighter or leaving at four in the morning so the kids sleep away the largest part of a four- or five-hour ride. Telling the kids they get 50 cents for every goat they see is also a brilliant maneuver.

The main point is this: don't ever leave on a long "vacation" with the kids without putting on your thinking cap first. Have the 1-2-3 and a few other tactics in your hip pocket, because you're going to need them.

8

Variations: Sibling Rivalry, Tantrums and Pouting

There are three problems that kids present that require some minor modifications in the 1-2-3. These are sibling rivalry, temper tantrums and pouting.

Sibling Rivalry

When you have more than one child acting up, how are you going to handle the situation? There are several important rules that you should follow:

1. *Count both kids.* When the children are fighting, you should count both of them 90 percent of the time or so. Why? Because kids are tricky, and it is often very hard to tell who started the fight—even if you are right there. Have you ever been driving in the car with the kids in the back seat and you hear, "Mom, he's looking at me again!"? Who started that one? There's no way to tell. So you count both children, unless one is the obvious, unprovoked aggressor. But be careful.

2. *Never ask the world's stupidest question.* Every parent knows what that is: "What happened?" or "Who started it?" What do you expect to hear, a version of George Washington's "I cannot tell a lie"? All you get

is the kids blaming one another and yelling a lot. About the only time you really need to ask anything is if you think someone might be physically injured.

3. *Don't expect an older child to act more mature during a fight.* It doesn't even matter if the two kids are eleven years old and four years old. Don't say to the eleven-year-old, "She's only a baby; can't you put up with a little teasing once in a while?" That's loading the gun of the four-year-old, who will be sure to take advantage of it.

Imagine for a second that your eleven-year-old son comes up to you one day and says, "I want to ask you a question."

"Go ahead," you say.

"How come I always get a ten-minute time out, and Miss Shrimp over there only has to go for five minutes?"

"Because the rule in our house," you say, "is one minute of time out for each year of your life."

"WELL THAT'S THE DUMBEST THING I EVER HEARD OF!"

"That's 1."

This child doesn't want to talk and he doesn't really want information. He wants a fight, but don't get sidetracked into a useless argument. Count attacks and discuss discussions.

What if the kids have a fight and they share the same room? It's not a real brilliant idea to send two fighting children to the same place. Send one to his room and the other to an alternate time-out room. Then for the next rest period reverse the places. If they fight on the way to the rooms, extend the time outs by five or ten minutes.

Temper Tantrums

The problem with a temper tantrum is simple: what if the time out is up but the child's not done with the tantrum? The answer is also simple: the time out doesn't start until the tantrum is over. So if it takes the youngster fifteen minutes to calm down, the rest period starts after fifteen minutes. And if it takes the kid two hours to calm down (could be a room-wrecker), the time out starts after two hours. Don't stick your head in the room every ten minutes and tell the child to quiet down. Just leave him alone.

The only children we don't use the temper tantrum variation for are the two- and three-year-olds. They don't seem to get the idea, so just let them out after a couple of minutes and see what happens. If they still don't quiet down, leave them in a little longer the next time.

Pouting

Pouting is a very passive behavior designed to make you feel guilty. If you do wind up feeling guilty, that's really more your problem. Why should you feel bad for doing what you're supposed to do as a parent? You shouldn't.

So if you discipline a child and she gives you the ultimate martyr look, just turn around and walk away. The only time to do something different is if you get what we call an "aggressive pouter." That's a child who follows you all over the place to make sure you don't miss a minute of the sour face. If she does that, "That's 1."

9

Getting Started:
The Kickoff Conversation

Getting started with the 1-2-3 is pretty easy, but don't put a lot of stock in the impact of your initial conversation with the kids. Plenty of children don't really get the idea until you've been counting for a while, and after they've been to their rooms a few times.

So, even though it's a bit too much like little adult stuff, give the kids the benefit of the doubt and tell them what you'll be doing. If both parents are living at home, Mom and Dad should sit down with the children in the two-to-twelve-year range and say something like:

"Listen, you guys know there are times when you do things we don't like. From now on we're going to do something a little different. When we see you doing something you're not supposed to, we'll say, 'That's 1.' That's like a warning, and it means you're supposed to stop. If you don't stop, we'll say, 'That's 2.' If you still don't stop, we'll say, 'That's 3, take 5 [or however many minutes for your age].' That means you have to go to your room for a time out or a kind of rest period. When you come out, we don't talk about what happened unless it's really necessary. We just forget it and start over.

"If the thing you're doing is real bad to start with, like swearing at us or hitting, we'll say, 'That's 3, take 10 or 15.' That means there aren't any warnings except that one, and you just go straight to your room. Do you have any questions?"

Expect the kids to sit there and look at you like you've gone off your rocker. Some kids will poke each other and exchange knowing glances, as if to say, "Well, it looks like Mom went to the library again and got another one of those books on how to raise us guys. Last time she stuck to it for about four days. I think if we stick together and hang tough, we should be running the house again inside of two weeks, right?"

Wrong. Don't expect them to be grateful or to look enlightened. Just stick to your guns, get going, and, when in doubt, count!

At this point of this book, you may feel that you're ready to start using the 1-2-3. Not so fast! If you began counting right now, you wouldn't be prepared for the fact that many children—about half—are not going to thank you for your efforts. Instead, they are going to engage in one or more of the Six Kinds of Testing and Manipulation. You've got to know what these are and how to handle them before you get going.

Part III

No Child
Will Thank You

10

The Six Kinds of
Testing and Manipulation

At this point, you are almost—but not quite—ready to start using the 1-2-3 for Stop behavior problems with your children. The reason you're not totally ready yet has to do with the fact that the kids will not thank you for your efforts to discipline them more effectively and make your house a happier place in which to live. In fact, as mentioned earlier, many children will test you immediately. They will get worse before they get better.

So you have to be ready for *Testing and Manipulation (T&M)*. These are the efforts of the frustrated child to weasel his way out of something, avoid discipline or sidetrack you in your efforts. Several things need to be remembered:

Testing occurs when the child is frustrated. You are not giving him what he wants; you are counting him; you are making him do homework or go to bed. He doesn't like this and hopes for a way out.

Testing, therefore, is purposeful behavior. The purpose of the child's testing and manipulation, obviously, is to get his way rather than have you impose your will on him. In fact, T&M can have two purposes, which may come in sequence.

A. The first purpose of testing and manipulation is for the child *to get what he wants*.

B. The second purpose of T&M kicks in if the first fails. If the child cannot get his way, he will try to get something else: *revenge*.

When using T&M, the child has a "choice" of six possible tactics. All six can serve the first purpose; five of the six can serve the second purpose.

All parents and teachers recognize these tactics. They have seen them many times. They also usually know which ones are used by which children. They may also recognize some of their own favorites, because adults use the same basic T&M methods that kids use.

Here are the six tactics that frustrated children use on their adult tormentors:

1. Badgering

Badgering is like the "Please, please, please" or "Why, why, why?" business. The child just keeps after you and after you and after you, trying to wear you down with repetition. "Just give me what I want and I'll shut up!" is the underlying message. "Mom! Mom! Mom! Mom! Mom!" Some kids sound like machine guns, and they can be amazingly persistent.

If the parent attempts to verbally respond to everything the child says every time he says it, Mom or Dad is in for a very long and frustrating evening. Many parents continue on a wild-goose chase looking for the right words or reasons to make the youngster be quiet.

2. Intimidation

Intimidation is an aggressive attack which often involves temper tantrums. The aggravated child may yell at you or otherwise storm around the house. Younger children may throw themselves on the floor, bang their heads, and kick around ferociously. Older kids sometimes get into swearing. They may also come up with arguments that accuse you of being unjust, illogical or simply a bad parent in general.

3. Threat

> "I'll never speak to you again!"
> "I'm going to kill myself!"
> "I'm not eating dinner and I won't do my homework!!"
> "I'm going to kill the parakeet!"
> "I'm running away from home!"

These are all examples of threats. The message is, something bad is going to happen to you unless you cease and desist from your ridiculous requests, restrictions or discipline at once.

4. Martyrdom

As opposed to threats, actually not talking, not eating dinner, or sitting in the closet for two hours may be examples of martyrdom.

"No one around here loves me anymore. Might as well find another family to live with."

Crying, pouting and looking sad or teary can also be effective. The goal, obviously, is to make the parent feel guilty, and martyrdom is surprisingly effective. Many Moms and Dads have a "guilt button" the size of the state of Wyoming! All the kids have to do is push it, and then *they* run the house.

The first four tactics—Badgering, Intimidation, Threat and Martyrdom—share a common, underlying dynamic: the child, without quite knowing what he's doing, is saying to the parent, "Look, you're making me uncomfortable by not giving me what I want. Now I'm making you uncomfortable with all this harping at you, temper tantrums, ominous statements and feeling sorry for myself. *Now that we're both uncomfortable, I'll make you a deal: you call off your dogs and I'll call off mine."*

Sounds good, right? If you do give in and give them what they want, you are almost guaranteed that the T&M will stop immediately. The problem, then, is who's running your house? It certainly isn't you; it's the kids. All they have to do in a difficult situation is get out their big guns and they've got you.

5. Butter Up

The fifth tactic takes a different approach. Instead of making you feel uncomfortable, the child tries to make you feel good.

"Gee, Mom, you've got the prettiest eyes of anybody on the block." Or, "I think I'll go clean my room. It's been looking kind of messy for the last three weeks. And after that maybe I'll take a look at the garage."

As opposed to the other kinds of testing, now the child is going to do something nice, often trying to *prevent* a frustrating event. Have you ever heard a parent say, "The only time he's ever good is when he wants something"? That's probably Butter Up, or what is also called "Sweetness and Light." This type of manipulation is sometimes tricky, because it's hard to tell it apart from genuine affection.

6. Physical Tactics

This is perhaps the worst. The frustrated child either physically attacks you, breaks things or runs away. Children don't usually start acting this way all of a sudden. Many of them have a long history of this kind of behavior, and the bigger they get, the scarier their behavior gets.

We took a brief survey once of parents, and later of teachers, asking which tactics they thought children used the most. Interestingly, both groups mentioned the same three: Badgering, Intimidation and—the overwhelming favorite—Martyrdom.

The $64,000 Question

Now comes the big question. Think of your kids, one at a time, and ask yourself, "Does this child have one—or perhaps two—tactics that he or she uses very frequently or even all the time?" If your answer is yes, this is probably bad news. Why? Because the tactic most likely is working. People tend to repeat something because it works for them.

What does "it works" mean?

Remember the two purposes of testing and manipulation. First of all, the child may be successfully getting his way by using the tactic. How do you know if a child is getting his way by testing? It's obvious—you just give in to him. You turn the TV back on, stop counting, or don't make him do his homework or go to bed.

"It works" can also refer to the second purpose of T&M: *revenge*. How do you know if a child is effectively getting revenge? Think back to the No-Talking, No-Emotion Rules. If this child can get you all upset, or get you talking too much, she knows she's got you. You are uncomfortable and paying for your sins.

Let's say you want the homework done, and the child pulls #2 on you, Intimidation. Yelling, screaming, banging things—the whole nine yards. Your response, however, is a *counter* temper tantrum. You get more upset than your daughter did! Final score: Child 5, Parent 2. She's got you: the small, inferior part of the youngster got the big splash from the larger, "more powerful" adult.

Or say your child—when asked to go to bed—does a #4 (Martyrdom): "Well, it's obvious that nobody around here loves me anymore. I might as well hitch the next freight to Iowa and find a family more compatible with my basic needs" [touch of #3, Threat]. You feel frightened, guilty. You are certain that unloved children grow up to be homeless people or serial killers.

You sit the youngster down on your lap, and for a half hour tell him how much you love him, how much Dad and the dog love him, etc., etc. You have just been had by tactic #4, Martyrdom. Unless you are a grossly neglectful or abusive parent, your kids know that you love them, and by all means tell them that you love them.

But never tell them that you love them when they're pulling a #4 on you.

Doing It Right

Now, let's say you're learning the 1-2-3 and you're toughening up a bit. Your ten-year-old child wants to go to a friend's house at 9 p.m. on a school night. You say no, and the following scene occurs:

"Why not? Come on, just this once!" (Badgering)

"Can't do it."

"You never give me anything around here!" (Martyrdom)

"I don't think you're too underprivileged."

"I promise I'll clean the garage later." (Butter Up)

"The garage is OK now. I just did it."

"This stinks—I HATE YOUR GUTS!" (Intimidation)

"Sorry."

The child tries to hit you on the arm. (Physical)

"Watch your step, pal."

"Oh, please, PLEASE, oh, come on, it's not so late." (Badgering)

"No way, José—it's outta bounds for you."

"If you don't, I'm gonna split for good." (Threat)

This is good! Why? Because something constructive is happening. The child is fishing around, switching tactics and probing for your weak spot. He can't find it. You are sticking to your guns and not only that, you are remaining fairly calm in spite of the aggravation.

There is one thing wrong with this example, however. It has to do with how you handle testing and manipulation. You would not let the child switch tactics that many times. Why? Because if you look at the original six T&M tactics, five of them are Stop behaviors (except for Butter Up). So if a child were pushing you this much, you would count him.

Remember the Twinkie example? This is how it should be handled:

"Yeah, but I want one." (Badgering)

"That's 1."

"You never give me anything!" (Martyrdom)

"That's 2."

"This is so stupid! I'm going to kill myself and then run away from home!!" (a "2-3" pattern: Intimidation plus Threat)

"That's 3, take 5."

Remember: with the exceptions of Butter Up and passive pouting, testing and manipulation should be counted.

What to Expect

We mentioned before that when you start the 1-2-3, the kids would fall into two categories: immediate cooperators and immediate testers.

The immediate cooperators you simply enjoy. The immediate testers, however, will get worse at first. When you try to take away the power of their favorite T&M method, they will initially respond in one of two ways. They may *"up the ante"* for a particular tactic, making it much worse. The volume and length of a tantrum, for example, may double. Their other response can be to *switch tactics*, perhaps trying new ones or returning to others they haven't used for years. Tactic switching is aggravating, but remember that it is almost always a sign that you are doing well at being firm.

Keep your mouth shut. Count when necessary. Eventually tactic escalation and tactic switching will diminish, and the result will be that the youngster begins to accept your discipline without having a major cow every time. You then have won the battle. You are the parent, they are the children, and your home is a more peaceful place.

Some kids, after doing well for a while, later become sort of "delayed testers." Delayed testing can come when the novelty of the new system wears off, the youngsters begin to realize that they aren't getting their way anymore, or your routine gets disrupted by travel, visitors, illness, new babies or just plain time.

Delayed testing can be somewhat disillusioning, because "the kids were so good before!" You may feel like the whole system is falling apart, or that it was too good to be true.

Fortunately, the remedy is not far away. Read this book again, discuss its suggestions with your spouse, then get back to basics: No Talking, No Emotion, be gentle but aggressive and when in doubt count. Things should shape up fairly quickly.

11

Counting in Action

Here are some examples of the 1-2-3 in action, with brief commentary on how well Mom, Dad or teacher did in handling the situation.

General Stop Behavior

Mark, three years old, is picking up an old cigarette butt from the ash tray and looking at it quizzically.

> "No, Mark, put that down."
> (Mark picks up another one.)
> "Mark, that's 1."
> (Mark just stands there, holding the cigarettes.)
> "That's 2."
> (Mark drops the cigarettes.)

Comment: Good job, short and sweet. It's much easier for the toddler to focus on and to understand the crisp instruction. "Come on now, honey, that's yucky and you'll get your hands all dirty..." is more confusing and invites the alternative of testing and manipulation.

Requests

Eight-year-old Tom asks his mother if he can use his Dad's electric jig saw.

"I don't think so. You better wait till Daddy's home."
"Oh come on, Mom. I know how to do it."
"No, I think it's too dangerous."
"There's nothing else to do." (Badgering, Martyrdom)
"I said no. That's 1."
"THAT'S 1! THAT'S 2! THAT'S 3! THAT'S 12! THAT'S
20! THAT'S STUPID!" (Intimidation)
"That's 2."
"Didn't know you could count that high." (Intimidation)
"That's 3, take 10 and add 5 for the mouth."
"Gee, I'll need a calculator for this one."

Mom moves toward Tom to escort him if necessary, but he goes to his bedroom.

Comment: One explanation and then count. Mom also adds five for the smart mouth, and she has the presence of mind to stay cool in spite of the insult. When her son doesn't go to the rest period right away, she also does not get caught up in a stupid argument or little-adult conversations.

Interrupting

Mom and Dad are having an important private conversation on the couch. Seven-year-old Michelle jumps in between them.

"Hi, guys!"
"Hi, honey. Listen, Mom and Dad have to talk about something
very important for a few minutes, so you go play for a little
bit."
"I wanna be here with you. I promise I won't listen."
"No, dear. Come on now, you go and play."
"I don't have anything to do." (Badgering)
"Listen, young lady. We're not going to tell you again!"

"THERE'S NOTHING ELSE FOR ME TO DO!" (Intimidation)

"Do you want a spanking!?"

(Michelle starts crying.) (Martyrdom)

"OK, that's 1."

(Michelle leaves, crying.)

Comment: Pretty sloppy job by Mom and Dad. They only get around to counting after ridiculous attempts at persuasion, threatening a spanking, and risking World War III for nothing. They eventually recover and count.

Arguing

Eleven-year-old Jeff asks:

"Can I go out after dinner to play?"

"No, dear, you still have homework to do," says Mom.

"I'll do it when I come back in, right before bed."

"That's what you said last night, honey, and it didn't work. Remember?"

"Oh, please Mom. I promise!" (Badgering, Butter Up)

"Get your homework done first, and then you can go out. If you work hard, it shouldn't take more than a half hour."

"Why can't I just go out now!? I'll DO MY STUPID HOME-WORK!" (Intimidation)

"That's 1."

"I can't wait to grow up so I can go in the army. It's got to be more fun than living in this dump." (Martyrdom)

"That's 2."

"All right, all right, all right." (Jeff goes to start his homework.)

Comment: Mom did very well here. She tried a little negotiating, but when that didn't work she didn't get caught up in a useless argument or try to explain why her house wasn't the same as the military.

Classroom Misbehavior

Margaret is a child who occasionally takes an experimental approach to learning. Today she is attempting to write her language arts assignment on a piece of paper, but she is using an orange magic marker. Her teacher, Mrs. Simpson, notices and suggests a different approach.

> "Margaret, the assignment can't be done like that."
> "Why not?"
> "Don't you have a pen or a pencil?"
> "What's wrong with a magic marker?" (Badgering)
> "You know what's wrong with it. You know better than
>   that."
> "I think it looks OK." (Badgering)
> "Listen, I'm not going to tell you again. It's not acceptable like
>   that."
> "I can read it." (Badgering)
> "That's 1."
> "Oh, for pete's sake!" (Margaret gets out a pencil.)

Comment: In an obviously ridiculous situation, Mrs. Simpson gets into too much talking in the beginning, but then catches herself.

Sibling Rivalry I

Nine-year-old John and his seven-year-old sister Suzie are best of friends and best of enemies. They are playing with Legos on the living room floor. Dad is watching the football game on TV and so far is amazed the kids are getting along so well, but the fun is about to end.

> "Suzie, I need another wheel for my tank," says John sweetly.
> "No, John, I've got it on my wagon," says Suzie nervously.
> (Dad squirms in his chair. It's fourth-and-goal for the good guys.)
> "Lemme just use one wheel now. I'll give it back to you later,"
>   suggests brother.
> "No, my wagon needs four wheels," replies sister.
> "Your wagon looks stupid!"
> "Dad, John's gonna take one of my wheels and I had them
>   first!"
> (Dad's team had to try for a field goal and it was blocked. Dad is
>   not pleased.)

"Both of you, knock it off!"

"She doesn't need to hog all the wheels. There aren't enough
   for me to make what I want, and they're my Legos."

"But I made this first!"

"OK, kids, that's 1 for both of you."

"She's an idiot." (John smashes his creation and leaves.)

Comment: Not too bad. Perhaps Dad should have counted sooner instead of saying "Knock it off!" Should Dad have counted John for smashing his tank or badmouthing his sister? Some parents would count these behaviors, but others wouldn't because the tank was John's (and it can be rebuilt). John may also be doing the right thing by leaving the situation.

Dog Teasing

Four-year-old Michael has the dog backed into a corner and pushed up against the wall. The dog, normally patient, is starting to snarl. Mom intervenes.

"Michael, don't tease the dog, honey."

(Michael giggles and continues pushing the dog against the wall.)

"That's 1."

"No! I wanna pet him." (Dog snarls again.)

"That's 2."

"I WANNA PET HIM!" (Intimidation) (Continues torturing.)

"That's 3. Upstairs."

(Michael falls on floor, releasing the dog, but yelling and crying.
Mom drags the unwilling body to the bedroom for time out.)

Comment: Couldn't have done it better. No talking while "escorting" the child to the rest period.

Potential Spontaneous Sleepovers

"Can I have a friend sleep over tonight?"

"I don't think so, it's already eight-thirty."

"You let Jimmy have someone last night."

"That was because he asked a week ago."

"Come on, Mom, it's not too late." (Badgering)

"No, dear. Not this time."

"We'll be real quiet and won't stay up late." (Badgering, Butter Up)

(Mom says nothing, but scowls.)

"I never get to do anything." (Martyrdom)

"You never get to do anything? Oh, really? Where did I take you today? Tell me."

"That wasn't any fun anyway!" (Indimidation, Martyrdom)

"Well apparently nothing I do is good enough for you, young lady."

"ALL I WANT IS TO HAVE JULIE SLEEP OVER!"

"YOU LISTEN TO ME! I'M SICK OF THIS!" Etc., etc., etc.

Comment: Super bad news. Did the child's Martyrdom push the guilt button and then trigger an angry overreaction?

Sibling Rivalry II

Sean, 9, and Tammi, 11, are getting into it while trying to play Scrabble in the living room. Dad is washing dishes in the kitchen.

"It's my turn."

"No it isn't. You lost it 'cause you took so long."

"Give me that. I was going to pick up that one!"

"You scratched me!"

"I did not, you idiot! You started it!"

"You're so dumb it isn't funny."

(Dad enters.) "What's going on here?"

"She's cheating!"

"I am not, lamebrain, you're too slow!"

"Be quiet, both of you! Tell me what happened."

(General yelling and chaos follow the ill-fated inquiry.)

"OK, that's 1 for both of you."

(General yelling and chaos continue.)

"That's 2."

(Sean dumps the Scrabble board over, grabs a bunch of letters, and throws them at the piano.)

"Sean, that's 3, take a rest for 10."

Comment: Dad recovered pretty well after asking the world's dumbest question. He should have started counting earlier.

Summertime Boredom

It's August 3rd, school is still three weeks off, it's hot, and three kids are at home today. Mom doesn't know how long she'll last. Jimmy starts the whining first.

"There's nothing to do."

"Why don't you guys go down to the pool?"

"We just went there yesterday. And it's too hot."

"Why don't you play that new Nintendo game?"

"Nah."

"Why don't you walk to Alaska?"

"What?"

"Just kidding." (Mom laughs.)

"Mom, it's not funny!"

"Well, don't go giving me a hard time about it. Everything I suggest isn't good enough for your highness. I'm not the entertainment committee around here, so find something yourself and leave me alone!"

"You said you'd take us to Creature Castle at the new mall."

"Well, I can't today. I have too many things to do around here."

"See, we never get to do anything we want!"

Comment: Nice conversation if you're into self-torture. Counting should have been used much earlier. What is Mom expecting the child to say, "Thanks for the suggestions"?

Talking in Class

During geography, Sally and Marci start a conversation across the aisle. Mrs. Smith stops her discussion of crops in Argentina.

"Girls, I need your attention."
(The girls stop talking for thirty seconds, but then can't resist
finishing what they started.)
"Sally, Marci, that's 1."
(The girls stop talking.)

Comment: Crisp and to the point. Easier on the children's self-esteem than a lot of self-righteous criticism.

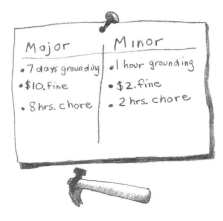

Major	Minor
• 7 days grounding	• 1 hour grounding
• $10. fine	• $2. fine
• 8 hrs. chore	• 2 hrs. chore

12

The Major/Minor System

Suppose your neighbor comes over on a summer day and tells you that your nine-year-old son just put a rock through his garage window. Deliberately. That's obviously Stop behavior, but it wouldn't make much sense to run to the back door and say, "Greg, that's 1." Certainly, "That's 3, take 5" would also seem be too mild. Some punishment is called for, but you still want to avoid a lot of excess talking and emotion that will make things worse.

More Serious Stop Behavior

From time to time, situations come up that are too serious for the 1-2-3 but still require some action on your part to train the kids not to repeat them. Included in this list are lying, stealing, serious fights, major behavioral problems at school, breaking things, losing things, not coming home, and so on. Fortunately, there is a very simple punishment system that you can set up to handle these problems well, with a minimum of upset. It's called the Major/Minor System.

You start the Major/Minor System by simply classifying any type of

Stop behavior as either Major or Minor, depending upon how serious you think it is. (The "Very Minor" things you're already handling with the 1-2-3.) Actually, it's often helpful to have a Major/Medium/Minor system so things aren't so black-and-white.

Once you have come up with your classifications, decide upon a punishment for each category, and dish out that punishment each time the offense occurs. This process saves a lot of effort and deliberation, and also lets the kids know beforehand what the consequences are for certain behavior. Typical punishments include groundings, fines, restrictions of such privileges as TV or computer time, and extra work around the house.

The punishments for Major offenses are greater than the punishments for Medium ones, and Medium consequences are bigger than those for Minor problems. Keep in mind that Minor offenses are still more serious than countable things such as arguing, yelling, teasing, whining and so on.

One family, for example, set up the following system for their nine-year-old son:

Major Offenses

Stealing, fighting, breaking something valuable, coming home more than three hours late, playing with fire

Medium Offenses

Coming home one to three hours late, lying

Minor Offenses

Coming home less than one hour late, losing or breaking something valued at less than $10

Note that not all possible misbehaviors are listed; these are simply the things these parents were having trouble with. They then set up the following consequences and agreed that for all but Major offenses their son could pick the punishment.

Major Consequences

Seven days grounding; $10 fine or pay back double the value of stolen article; no TV or computer for two weeks; eight hours work around the house

Medium Consequences

Three days grounding in room; $5 fine; four hours of chores

Minor Consequences

One hour grounding in room; $2 fine; two hours work around the house

You don't need to set up the system unless you already have some specific problems. When a problem occurs, simply categorize it and determine the consequence. No yelling or screaming by Mom and Dad is allowed, of course, though a *short* explanation may be in order. For each misbehavior, one (not all) of the possible punishments listed is administered. And, as mentioned before, sometimes the child can pick which one he wants.

You can adjust the Major/Minor System after you set it up, but be careful not to make punishments so harsh that they backfire. One family, for example, had a system like the one described above. Then one day they found out that their kid had stolen a bike! The Major punishments didn't seem big enough for this act, so they told the boy he was grounded for a year. This response will not work because it will be impossible to enforce. A better punishment would be grounding for a month and pay back the value of the bike.

What if the youngster does something that you didn't put on the original Major/Minor lists? You just classify it as Major or Minor and then give the corresponding punishment. If you've been having a real problem with repeated offenses, you can also make a chart that keeps track of the number of days in a row that are free of trouble. If the problems continue, it might be time for evaluation and counseling with a professional.

Caution

A few more tips about the Major/Minor plan:

First, it can't be used effectively with two-to-four year olds. They won't get the idea. They also don't usually present major problems like those we're discussing.

Second, it's a good idea to write down the plan—and perhaps even sign it—so everyone remembers exactly what it is.

Third, you usually don't need to do the Major/Minor unless you've already been having a fair amount of trouble with a child. If your youngster is basically a good kid and rarely gets into trouble, then one day is two hours late for dinner or gets into a fight, you want to find out what happened first. Then, if you think it was bad judgment or largely accidental on his part, a straightforward warning not to repeat the action may be enough.

Fourth, bigger problems make you madder. Keep explanations short and sweet, and be sure to active listen (covered later, Chapter 26) when you need more information from your child. Blowing your stack can ruin the effectiveness of whatever consequences you—or your child—select.

13

Lying

It's the truth. Kids will lie from time to time, which drives some parents crazy. The school calls at one o'clock to tell you that your ten-year-old son, Tom, got into a fight with a boy named Davey Smith at lunch. At 3:45 p.m. Tom comes home. The conversation then goes like this:

"How was your day?" you ask.
"Good, great sandwich you made me for lunch."
"Speaking of lunchtime, how did it go?" you inquire.
"Fine, we played baseball."
"Anything unusual happen?
"Not that I can think of."
"OK, listen, young man. You're lying to me. I got a call from the school today...etc., etc."

The parent is "cornering" the youngster. Got to find out what really happened *and* see if he'll tell the truth. Is this the right way to handle the situation?

Two Kinds of Lying

There are basically two kinds of lying. The first is making up stories that are designed to impress other people and build one's ego. The second— and by far the most common—is lying to get out of or avoid trouble. For example, kids often will lie about homework so they don't have to do it, or because they forgot to bring their books home. They may also deny having gotten into a fight or having stolen or broken something.

When it comes to dealing with lying, parents should remember not to treat the act as if it were the equivalent of homicide or adultery. It certainly isn't a good thing to do, but it's not the end of the world. Far too many parents get so upset about lying that they lead the child to believe that he is a horrible person.

What Should You Do?

A primary rule is *don't badger or corner children!* Imagine you give a child the third degree about whether or not he has homework. He denies it six times and then finally, after your seventh question, he admits that he has some. What has happened? By this time, of course, you are furious. More important, however, you also have given your child six times to practice lying! You may think to yourself, "Sooner or later he'll realize he can't fool me and he'll give up." Wrong. Many children will continue to take the easy way out: they will simply attempt to become better liars.

Look at it this way: you either know the truth or you don't. If you don't know what is going on, ask once and don't badger. It's a good idea here not to ask "impulsively," meaning on the spur of the moment. Many kids simply respond back impulsively. They lie, but their real desire is just to end the conversation, get rid of you, and stay out of trouble.

If you are going to ask, you might say something like, "I want you to tell me the story of what happened, but not right now. Think about it a while and we'll talk in fifteen minutes." If he tells you the story and you find out later that the child lied, punish him for whatever the offense was as well as for the lie (see the Major/Minor System in Chapter 12). No lectures or tantrums. Deal with the problem and try to fix things—as much as you can—so that lying does not seem necessary to the child. If he continually lies about homework, for example, work out some kind of communication with the teacher, such as a daily assignment sheet. Then use the tactics described in Chapter 17.

If you do know what has happened, tell him what you know and deal with it. If he has done something wrong that you know about, simply punish him reasonably for that and end the conversation with, "I'm sure you'll do better next time."

Some parents still prefer to ask a child what happened—even when they already know what it was. This is OK if you do it right. You should say something like, "I got a call from the school today about an incident at lunch. I'm going to ask you to tell me the story, but not right now. I want you to think about it for a while, then when you're ready you can tell me, but remember I already pretty much know what happened."

Lying is not good, but it certainly isn't the end of the world either. It happens from time to time. It doesn't mean that your kids don't love you or that they are bound to grow up to become professional criminals. Over the years, however, frequent emotional overreactions on your part— combined with badgering and cornering—can produce an Accomplished Liar.

Part IV

Encouraging
Good Behavior

14

The Six
Start Behavior Tactics

We will now turn our attention to managing Start behavior—the positive things you want to encourage children to do. This category includes doing schoolwork, going to bed, eating, cleaning rooms, practicing musical instruments, and getting up and out in the morning.

It's a good idea, when beginning this program, to use the 1-2-3 first for a week to ten days or so before worrying about Start behavior. If you try to do the whole program at once, it's a little too complicated and too much to keep straight. It will also be considerably easier to get the kids to do the good things if you have first gotten back in control of the house.

When you are using your Start behavior tactics, don't be surprised by the kids' testing and manipulation. Remember, a child is not going to thank you for encouraging him to clean his room. If you have worked on counting negative behavior first, you will have had a fair amount of experience in dealing with Stop behavior before you tackle the task of getting the kids to do the good things.

There are six Start behavior tactics you can consider using. It is important, however, to keep in mind several general rules:

A. You can always try a Simple Request first (just as you can with Stop behavior). Ask the child to clean her room or tell her it's time to start practicing the clarinet. If she doesn't respond, though, don't get caught up in attempts at persuasion using little-adult ideas.

B. Start behavior tactics can often be combined. You don't have to use just one for each type of problem. You can be somewhat creative.

C. Angry people make noise; happy ones do not. We all suffer from a biological curse that motivates us to say something to our kids when we're angry. Then we tend to keep quiet when we're feeling things are going OK. The result is not good. Family members can start feeling they're just a pain in the neck if we don't regularly try to hand out some reinforcing or appreciative comments. The first Start behavior strategy (Sloppy PVF) is a good antidote for this curse.

D. Train them or be quiet! In the 1-2-3 program there is a method or way of handling just about every kind of problem your kids can throw at you. So use them! If the child isn't cleaning his room, train him to clean it. Otherwise, be quiet, clean it yourself, or close the door and don't look. *Training, however, does not mean nagging, arguing, yelling or hitting.*

With these rules in mind, let's take a look at the six tactics you will use to get the kids to do what they're supposed to.

Sloppy PVF

Sloppy Positive Verbal Feedback, otherwise known as praise or reinforcement, should be dished out on a regular basis. Like voting in Chicago, Sloppy PVF should be done early and often. If you look, you shouldn't have trouble finding something to reinforce. And once you've gotten the kids going with some other Start behavior tactic, positive reinforcement can help keep it going. The "sloppy" refers to the fact that you don't reinforce everything all the time. In fact, some irregularity to your praise is probably a good idea.

Here are some examples of Sloppy PVF:

"Thanks for doing the dishes."
"You started your homework all by yourself!"
"You kids did a good job of getting along during the movie."

"I think you got ready for school in record time this morning!"

"Good job on that math test, John."

"That's wonderful! I can't believe it! How on earth did you do that?!"

Sloppy PVF should be "tailored" to the child. Some kids like rather elaborate, emotional verbal reinforcement, like the last example above. Other kids are embarrassed by it, and may prefer statements like the second-to-last example. Pay attention to your child's reactions to see if you can tell what he prefers.

How do you keep offering praise and encouragement on a regular basis? As mentioned before, this task is surprisingly difficult, since most of us tend to shut up when we are content. Here are two suggestions. First, see if you can make two positive comments for every one negative comment. These remarks don't have to be made at the same time, of course. They can be said later. If the two-to-one ratio idea doesn't appeal to you, a second strategy is to have a quota system: each day you make a deal with yourself that you will make at least five positive comments to each child (consider doing the same with your spouse!).

Kitchen Timers

Kitchen timers are a great help for many Start behaviors, such as home-work, getting up in the morning, eating and going to bed. They can also be used to time the time outs themselves. You can even take timers in the car with you. Kids, especially the younger ones, have a natural tendency to want to beat the things.

You could say to a five-year-old, for example, "You've got three things in the kitchen I would like picked up and put in your room. I'm setting the timer for ten minutes and I'll bet you can't beat it!"

The response will often be, "Oh yes I can!" and the youngster will be off to do the job. You could take this same tack with an eleven-year-old, but you would phrase your request in a more matter-of-fact manner. If the child doesn't respond by picking up the things, you can later use the Docking System (see below).

Kitchen timers are also helpful because they are not testable, i.e., they don't respond when a child uses one or more of the T&M tactics, such as Badgering, Intimidation or Martyrdom. Timers just keep ticking.

The Docking System

The idea of the Docking System is like docking wages: if you don't do the work, you don't get paid. This plan, of course, requires that the kids have an allowance. You can consider starting an allowance with children five or older. The payment doesn't have to be anything large, but it's a good idea to have half of it based on doing things around the house (e.g., cleaning his room, chores, homework). The other half is simply given to the child, partly so you are sure you have some leverage when it comes time to use the Docking procedure.

Let's imagine you've been having the typical parent-child discussion about getting a dog. The child wants the dog, but you wisely object that he probably won't take care of it on his own. Let's assume you get the dog (because you want one, too).

What do you do? You tell the child what the deal will be. He's eleven and gets about $3 per week allowance. You want the dog fed by six o'clock each night. If he feeds the dog by then, fine (use Sloppy PVF). If he doesn't get to the dog by six, you have good news and bad news. The good news is that you will feed the dog. The bad news is that you charge to feed other people's dogs, and for this mutt it will be 15 cents per feeding taken off the $3 allowance. The child agrees.

Here's how it might go. The first night it's ten after six, there's no child around, and the dog's looking hungry. You wait. At quarter after your son comes running in asking if you fed the dog. You say, "No." He says, "Good!" and feeds the dog. You give him some Sloppy PVF—he was only a little bit late and it is the first night.

The second night it's twenty after six and you finally feed the hungry animal at your feet. At six-thirty the boy comes running in:

"Did you feed the dog?"
"Yes, I did, and I had to charge you fifteen cents off your
    allowance."
"WELL, WHAT DID YOU DO THAT FOR?!" (Yelling)

"That's 1."

This is not going to be a discussion. It's simply one version of testing tactic No. 2, Intimidation, and it should be counted. In this kind of situation, it's extremely difficult to resist the temptation to get into little-adult types of comments, such as, "Do you remember when we bought this stupid mutt for you? What did you say, huh? You said, 'I'll feed the dog every single night. No problem!' Right! Well, here we are on only the second night and I'm already feeding your dog! I'm sick of doing everything around here and you kids are going to have to learn..."

What you're saying may be absolutely correct, but it will do no good and cause some harm. Be quiet and let the money do the talking. If money doesn't seem to have much clout with the child, take minutes off his TV time or use some other reasonable consequence.

Natural Consequences

Here you let the big, bad world teach the child what works and what doesn't. There are times when your staying out of some problems is the best approach. Suppose you have a fourth grader who is taking piano lessons for the first time. She is not practicing as she should, however, and can't sleep at night because she's worrying that her piano teacher will be mad.

What should you do? Nothing. Some piano teachers are very good at getting uncooperative kids to tickle the ivories on a regular basis between lessons. If after a few weeks, the teacher's efforts don't work, you may want to try other Start behavior tactics, such as using the timer or charting. But leave the situation alone for a while in the beginning.

Or, suppose you have a sixth grader. He's supposed to make his own lunch, with stuff that you buy, and then brown bag it to school. It seems like every day he is yelling at you about how hungry he was at lunch with nothing to eat. What should you do? Relax, and give him some encouragement by saying something like, "I'm sure you'll do better tomorrow." If his Badgering continues, it should be counted.

Another example of a good time to use natural consequences? Winter-time dress. All parents know that junior high and high school students think there are federal laws against zipping or buttoning up their coats in the winter. Let them feel a little cold if they're not dressed properly, and avoid starting the day with the obvious, aggravating lecture.

Charting

Charting involves using something like a calendar which you can put on the refrigerator door or on the back of the child's bedroom door. Put the days of the week across the top, and down the side list the different tasks the child will be working on, such as cleaning her room, getting to bed, and feeding the dog. If the child completes the task to your satisfaction, you indicate this on the chart with stickers for the little kids (ages 3 to 8) and grades or numbers (A-F, 5-1) for the older children.

Here's what a chart might look like. This child is working on cleaning his room, brushing his teeth, and feeding the dog:

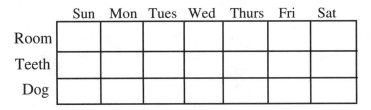

	Sun	Mon	Tues	Wed	Thurs	Fri	Sat
Room							
Teeth							
Dog							

Reinforcement with charting comes, hopefully, from both parental praise (Sloppy PVF) and the inherent satisfaction of doing a good job. These often work well to stimulate a child to do the job, but not always. Your child may just be a natural slob and a clean room means nothing to him. Or your little girl may be ADD and LD, and homework provides no satisfaction—but much frustration—for her.

In these cases you must go with *artificial reinforcers*—sometimes referred to as bribery. This is OK because some kids need something pleasant in order to help them overcome their aversion or indifference to a project. Reinforcers can be part of one's allowance, or special meals, or baseball cards, or staying up later at night occasionally. The best ideas are relatively small things that can be dished out frequently and in small pieces. Try to be as creative as possible in coming up with reinforcers. They certainly do not always have to be material. Some kids, for example, will work hard to earn minutes to stay up later at night, or to be able to do some special activity with one of their parents.

Keep the chart simple. Three or four things to work on at one time is enough; more gets too confusing. Also, build in "discontinuation criteria"—rules for determining when the chart is no longer necessary. You certainly are not going to do charting forever, and too often its effects can fade because Mom and Dad are simply getting tired of doing it. You might say, for example, that if the child gets good scores (define them precisely) for two weeks running, that item will be taken off the chart. When the child has earned his way off the chart entirely, it's time to go out for pizza and a movie to celebrate. If the child regresses, you can reinstate the chart.

The 1-2-3 (different version)

It may seem kind of odd, but the 1-2-3, which was earlier used for Stop behavior, can also be used for Start behavior, but only on one condition: what you want the child to do cannot take over two minutes. So if the child throws her coat on the floor after school, and you ask her to pick it up and she doesn't, just say, "That's 1." If she gets timed out, she goes and serves the time, and when she comes out, you ask her to pick it up again. If no cooperation, another time out follows. Keep this up until she gets the idea.

What if she is in a totally ornery mood and never gets the idea? Just switch to the Docking System. You hang up the coat for her, but you charge for your services. Keep the talking to a minimum, and count whining, arguing, yelling and other forms of hassling (T&M).

What can you use this version of the 1-2-3 for? Things like feeding the dog, brushing teeth or just "Would you please come here for a second?" might take less than two minutes. What should you *not* use the 1-2-3 for? Longer projects like homework, eating dinner, getting up and out in the morning, and so on.

When working on encouraging positive behavior, remember the rule that says, "Train them or be quiet." Also, be careful with what we call "spontaneous requests." Spontaneous requests are requests that parents make of their children on the spur of the moment—when the parent sees that the room is messy, or the clothes are still in the dryer, he or she asks the youngster—who is watching TV—to take care of the problem. The child reacts with hostility and then the parent says, "Why can't you do just this one little thing for me when we do everything all the time for you? What's the big deal? Now MOVE!"

In a way, parents are correct here, but they're also being very naive. No kid likes being interrupted. Spontaneous requests certainly can't be avoided, but they always *maximize irritability and minimize cooperation.* When asked to do something, is the child supposed to say, "Thanks for giving me this unanticipated opportunity to be of service"?

Not likely. Try to minimize spontaneous requests and maximize use of the six Start behavior tactics.

15

Up and Out
in the Morning

C lose to the top of the list for greatest Start behavior hassles is the problem of getting the kids up and out of the house in the morning. This is mostly a problem for grammar-school kids, though it can apply to preschoolers too. This situation often brings out the worst in everybody. Many people—both parents and kids—are naturally crabby in the morning, and there is the additional pressure of having to get someplace *on time*. The nervousness, nagging and emotional thunderstorms that result can easily ruin a parent's day.

For the kids, getting up and out in the morning involves a whole sequence of Start behaviors: out of bed on time, washing up, brushing teeth, making the bed, eating breakfast and leaving the house. What is required varies some from family to family, but it's basically the same job. Believe it or not, these awful morning situations can often be shaped up rather quickly using some of the principles outlined before.

No Talking and No Emotion still apply—even if you haven't had your first cup of coffee.

For the Little Ones

With most kids ages two to four, you'll have to help them get ready and supervise them closely. They just can't sustain the activity for that long. Use a lot of Sloppy PVF during the process.

For other children up to about age nine, using charting plus a kitchen timer can be very helpful. Stickers can be used (or numbers if the child prefers). The child's favorite sticker is earned for a super job of getting ready, and her next most favorite sticker for a good job. No sticker at all means "You blew it, better luck tomorrow."

If you are using the timer, the best sticker can be given for getting ready in a certain amount of time. Remember that doing well involves not only completing the required activities of washing and dressing, but also doing them as much as possible by oneself and without complaining. A lot of parents also find that not letting the kids watch TV until they're ready is a good idea. Some children also can't eat breakfast until they're ready, though you don't want to send them off to school hungry.

Desperate?

Once upon a time there was a mother who was getting more and more fed-up with her four-year-old's fooling around in the morning and never being ready for preschool. The boy was quite bright, but he just never seemed to get going. Whenever the car pool ride came, she was always dressing him at the last minute.

One day Mom finally decided she'd had it with the yelling and screaming and lack of cooperation. It was her day to drive the kids and, as usual, it was time to go—and her son was in his pajamas watching TV. So she did the ultimate: she took him to preschool in his pajamas. The amazed little fellow spent the whole morning of two and one-half hours with his peers—all the time dressed in his pajamas!

A much more relaxed Mom later reported that that was the last time she had any trouble getting her son ready for school.

Such a method is not for the faint-hearted. But neither is what we're about to suggest for older children.

Up and Out for Older Kids

For nine-year-olds and up, the program involves some semi-drastic alterations in the morning routine, which often shock the kids into changing.

First of all, it is important to realize that most of these kids want to go to school and/or they would be embarrassed if they didn't show up or were late. So if they dilly-dally around in the morning, they are going to have some trouble with someone in the car pool, or with the principal or teachers at school. Most kids don't want these kinds of hassles, so we use the threat of these natural consequences to shape them up.

Here's how it works. You explain to the kids that from now on it will be their job to get themselves up and out in the morning. *You will neither supervise them nor nag.* You can put out clothes for them the night before, if necessary. If you have been waking them up, go out and buy an alarm clock and show them how to use it.

You make it clear to the kids that getting up, getting dressed, washing up, eating breakfast, and leaving on time will be *their* job. If you wish, you can chart them on how well they do, but you cannot say anything to them while they are getting ready, other than casual conversation.

Many parents can't stand this—it drives them crazy to watch the kids fooling around at a late hour, so we ask these parents to take their coffee, retire to the bedroom, and not watch the impending disaster.

Breakfast is optional. You can put something out if that's your usual routine, but *you can't remind the kids to eat it.* Or they can just get their own if they want. Most children won't die from missing breakfast. When they leave, you say nothing about coats, hats or gloves, unless there is danger of frostbite.

If the kids fight, you can ignore it or count them if it gets too bad, but that's all. If it's close to time to leave, they may be timed out for only a couple minutes (or take away TV minutes for later).

What you are doing is teaching the kids some independence and invoking a sacred rule of psychology: Sometimes Learning the Hard Way is the Best Way to Learn. The lessons sink in more when kids get burned a few times than they do when they simply hear a lecture. So you have to be willing to *let the kids get burned.*

What does this mean? It means being late to school a few times, being embarrassed and having to explain to the principal or teacher what happened. It means suddenly realizing at 7:50 that you're not dressed and that Mom didn't remind you that your car pool ride or bus was coming at 8:00. It means getting to school and realizing you forgot your math book at home because you were late leaving. It means blowing your stack at your mother a few times because she's not nagging you anymore to get ready on time, or because she won't write you an excuse note.

These experiences have quite a bit of impact on most kids. If the parents are consistent, don't talk and let the kids get burned, the children will shape up in a few days. Then things will be much more peaceful at home in the morning and the kids will be much more responsible.

By the way, kids have four main ways of getting to school: car pool, bus, walking or riding bikes. When you are within walking distance of the school, the up-and-out program is the easiest. With car pools or bus, you may have to drive the kids if they don't make their connection. For most kids this isn't a problem—they don't get dependent on your driving all the time, especially if they're late. Remember not to lecture them on the way to school if you do have to drive them.

Say nothing.

If you're charting along with the program, use Sloppy PVF for good performances and review the chart at least once a week. You *can* discuss the problem—listen, give brief suggestions, modify things, etc.—at times other than when the kids are getting ready in the morning.

Skeptical?

Many parents, before using this procedure, think their kids will be indifferent to it. They think the kid really doesn't care whether or not he gets to school on time. Part of the reason they think this is because the kid has said so. *Never believe a child who says, "I don't care."* He usually means the opposite and is testing you.

If you are skeptical, try it out and see what happens. Most kids—not all, but most—will respond well. The most important rules are to shut up, stay out of it, and be willing to let the kid get burned more than once. If necessary, let the school know what you're doing. Most times, teachers and principals will cooperate with you, especially if you explain your purpose and label the procedure "independence training."

What if it doesn't work? You have some other Start behavior tools, remember? Try charting with artificial reinforcers or using the timer.

If it does work? Enjoy another cup of coffee—and the peace and quiet.

16

Cleaning Rooms
and Eating

C leaning bedrooms may be the chief cause of parent-child quarrels among all Start behavior problems. Many parents become absolutely enraged when they view the scenes of destruction and chaos in their kids' bedrooms:

> "Barbara, GET UP HERE RIGHT THIS MINUTE!"
> "What?"
> "LOOK AT THIS ROOM! I can't even see the CARPET!
>   How am I supposed to do your clothes?"

Kids are not naturally neat. Many—if not most—are natural slobs. The cleaning gene is missing from their chromosomal makeup. So they will have to be *trained* to clean their rooms. How can you accomplish that? By this time you shouldn't have to be reminded that you won't get them to do it by nagging or delivering the lecture, "The Five Reasons Why It's Easier on Me for You to Have a Clean Room."

Instead, you have several options. If you're creative, you can probably come up with several more. Here are some good ones.

Option 1: Close the Door and Don't Look

Having a clean room is not a life or death matter, and we know of no research that indicates that kids who didn't keep their rooms neat grow up to be homeless people or criminals or have a higher divorce rate. Besides, whose room is it? You don't have to live in it, so just ask the child to keep the door closed so you don't have to be aggravated. If you have a handicapped child or one who's very difficult anyway, why add one more hassle to your problems? You have bigger things to worry about.

Option 1 is quite legitimate, but there are two problems with it: 1) most parents find it unacceptable, and 2) what about dirty dishes and laundry left in the room?

If you don't want to use Option 1, more suggestions follow. As for dirty dishes and clothes, you can use other Start behavior tactics: the timer, charting or the 1-2-3 (if the dishes or clothes can be picked up in less than two minutes). Some parents whose kids are older simply tell the children that any clothes that don't make it to the laundry or hamper simply don't get washed. That's natural consequences.

The docking system can also be helpful. You go and get the dirty clothes or dishes from their room, but you charge them for your labor. You'll feel better about having to do it, but make sure you keep your mouth shut about the whole operation. And keep the fees reasonable.

Option 2: The Weekly Cleanup Routine

With this method, the kids have to clean their rooms only once a week, but according to your specifications. You might tell them that the following has to be done: pick up, clothes in hamper, make bed, etc. (no windows). A specific day is chosen, such as Saturday morning, and the child doesn't go out or do anything else until his room is done and you've checked him out. You can check him out on a chart if you wish.

Since cleaning the room is a Start behavior, you are rewarding the child right after the cleaning with both freedom and Sloppy PVF. Many parents have tried something like the Weekly Cleanup Routine, but they often ruin it by getting into a hassle with the child at checkout. Remember not to argue about what needs to be done, and try to make the specifications clear to begin with. For example:

"I'm done with my room. Can I go out now?"

"Your bed's not finished."

"Whatta ya mean? That's good enough."

(Mom turns to walk away.)

"What's the matter with it?"

"That's 1."

"Oh, for Pete's sake!!" (Goes to finish bed.)

This Mom had already explained before that the bed has to be neatly made, so there was no need for further talk. The kid starts testing using the Badgering tactic, and, after ignoring it once, Mom uses the 1-2-3. If the youngster winds up back in his room with a 3 count, that's fine, because he'll have five minutes to make his bed.

Option 3: Daily Charting

For parents who are more fastidious about cleanliness, the child's room can be charted every day using either the star system (for younger kids) or the 1-5 rating system (for older kids). The child can be informed that the rating will take place every night right before bed.

Keep in mind that you're probably asking for a lot of trouble trying to do this every day, so if you insist on doing this, be nice! Use a lot of Sloppy PVF if the job is done well, and don't expect perfection.

Option 4: The Kitchen Timer

The Close the Door and Don't Look method applies to the kids' rooms. It doesn't apply to the rest of your house! It does not mean the children can keep your kitchen, family room or dining room constantly piled up with all their things. Kitchen counters and dining room tables are such convenient dumping grounds.

The timer is helpful for cleaning rooms (including family rooms), especially when the job has to be done right away. If a surprise guest is coming over, you may not have much time to play around. When using the timer like this, it's perfectly OK to add an artificial reward if the room is done within a certain time, or even an artificial punishment if it's not. Use the Docking System if you feel you are getting stuck with everything.

Eating

Mealtimes can be particularly taxing when a family has one or more children. General fidgetiness plus a little sibling rivalry, plus a few other problems, sometimes make dinnertime a nightmare.

Oddly enough, many families seem to feel that there is a federal law that dictates that every family eat supper together each and every night of the year. This is the time, they say, for "family togetherness" and for each person to "share his or her day" with everyone else. Sometimes, however, it simply becomes the time for everyone to share their *hostility* toward everyone else. Tempers as well as appetites can be lost, and the whole affair becomes anything but pleasant and relaxing.

What can a parent do to improve this situation? One solution, obviously, is not to eat together every night. Though some people consider this sacrilegious, it sure beats fighting all the time. Now you only have to fight every other night! Seriously, sometimes you can feed the kids first or let them eat in front of the TV for once. Or let everyone eat wherever they want to, as long as they bring back their dishes. Then Mom and Dad eat in the kitchen or have a peaceful dinner together later.

Another approach when eating together—especially if the kids horse around too much at the table—is this: first get out a kitchen timer and set it for 20 minutes. Then tell everyone they have to finish in that time. If they do, they get their dessert. If they goof around, they get counted.

If they hit a count of three, they are timed out for five minutes while the 20 minute timer keeps on ticking. Don't do any prodding or nagging about eating, such as, "Come on now, don't forget the timer's ticking" or "Quit that goofing around and get down to eating, young man!" (How are you going to finish your own meal if you're talking all the time?)

What if the timer rings and they're not done? No dessert yet. The plate goes into the kitchen and onto the counter. After a half hour has expired, they have the opportunity to finish the meal if they wish. It can be nuked quickly in the microwave if necessary. If they don't ever eat the rest of it, fine, but no dessert. Some parents throw the rest of the dinner down the disposal when the timer hits 20 minutes, but this reaction seems a little harsh.

Stay on your toes when a hungry little tot who didn't finish her dinner puts the hit on you for some dessert later:

"I'm ready for my dessert now."
"You'll have to finish your dinner first, honey."
"It's all cold now."
"We'll just heat it in the microwave for a few seconds and it'll
   be good as new."
"I didn't like it anyway. I want just a little dessert."
"Now you know the rules, dear, you have to finish what's on
   your plate first. Remember, we didn't give you that much in
   the first place."
"I never get anything!"
"What are you talking about! Now that's enough of that! Either
   finish your dinner or stop bugging me."
"I hate you!"

An unfortunate waste of time and very hard on a relationship. It should have gone like this:

"I'm ready for my dessert now."
"You'll have to finish your dinner first, honey."
"It's all cold now."
"We'll just heat it in the microwave for a few seconds and it'll
   be good as new."
"I didn't like it anyway. I want just a little dessert."
"That's 1."
"Then I'll go to bed starving!" (Walks away)

Much better.

Think about dinnertime for a while. It should be a pleasant experience. With a little planning you can enjoy your evenings a lot more.

17

Homework and Practicing

omework hassles can make school nights miserable for the whole family. The typical scene involves junior sitting at the kitchen table staring out the window with a sour look on his face. His sister sits in the other room smugly watching TV. Mom and Dad check in the kitchen every five or ten minutes to badger the reluctant scholar.

For some families these battles can go on for two, three or four hours per night. People begin to dread the evening, relationships are strained severely, and the child in question learns to hate schoolwork more and more. There are no easy answers to the homework problem; children's needs vary depending upon their intelligence and the presence of handicaps such as learning disabilities and Attention Deficit Disorder. There are ways, though, of making things more tolerable and more productive.

What Not To Do

Don't go around asking the child every five minutes if he has homework or if he's started it yet. Instead try to pick the best time to start and stick with it—consistency is very important here.

Don't interrupt the youngster in the middle of his favorite TV show to tell him it's time to begin. There's *no* better way to get *no* cooperation. He should not start watching a show in the first place if it's going to overlap with his regular homework time.

Don't let the would-be student do work with the TV on. Believe it or not, a radio or stereo may be OK because it provides consistent background noise, but the television is always out to get your attention.

If you can avoid it, don't let the homework time change each day. One of the best ways of setting things up is to have the child come home, get a snack, goof off for about 30 to 45 minutes, and then sit down and try to finish his work before dinner. Then the whole evening is free.

What *to* do? Consider trying the following steps in order (you can combine them as you go), and be sure to use plenty of tailored Sloppy PVF along with whatever else you are doing.

Natural Consequences

If you are having trouble with homework for the first time—say with a fourth grader—consider using Natural Consequences first. That means do nothing. Keep your mouth shut and see if the child and the teacher can work things out. If this approach doesn't seem to be working after a few weeks, then go on to the next step.

Natural Consequences is obviously not the method to use if you have been having homework problems for years and years.

An Assignment Sheet

Assignment sheets or notebooks can be extremely helpful. They tell you exactly what work is due for each subject. Some schools have even instituted "Homework Hotlines," where forgetful but fortunate kids can call in after hours to find out what their assignments are.

The idea of the assignment sheet, of course, is that after the child does the work, parents can check it out against the list of items to be done. If this is the procedure you are considering, you must routinely include two basic principles: the "PNP Method" and the "Rough Checkout." Failure to do so will result in unnecessary misery.

The PNP Method

Suppose your daughter has just completed her midweek spelling pretest. There are ten words on the list and she spelled nine correctly and misspelled one. When she brings you her paper, your job, naturally, is to first point out to her the word she spelled wrong. Right?

Wrong! PNP stands for "Positive-Negative-Positive." Whenever any kid brings any piece of schoolwork to you, the first thing out of your mouth must be something good—some version of Sloppy PVF. Then, after saying something nice about the child's effort, you may throw in something negative, *if it's absolutely necessary*. Finally, you conclude your insightful remarks with something positive again.

Using the spelling pretest as an example, you would first say something like, "Gee, you spelled 'consideration' correctly. That's a pretty hard word. And you also got 'appearance' right. In fact, there's only one word on here that I can see you didn't get. Not bad."

You might stop here and try to kill her with suspense. See if she's dying to find out what the wrong word is. If she's not, you can tell her. Then end the conversation with another positive comment.

Remember the rule: every time she brings you some work to check, the first thing you say must be positive, even if it's only the fact that she brought the work to you. Kids will never want to bring you anything if your first response is consistently to shoot from the hip with criticism.

The Rough Checkout

The Rough Checkout idea is based on the fact that 8 p.m. is no time for scholastic perfection. You have worked all day, and your child has also put in just about the equivalent of a day on a full-time job —before she started her homework!

Unless there is some major indication to the contrary, if her work is anywhere near 80 per cent neat, correct and thorough, consider calling it a day. Let your youngster and teacher worry about the assignment tomorrow. This advice is doubly true for ADD or LD children who are already having a tough enough time with school. If, on the other hand, the child is generally a very good student (not potentially, but actually), you might consider raising the required percentage to 90 or more.

A mother once came in to my office reporting that her 12-year-old son seemed to be getting depressed, more irritable, and more distant from everyone in the family. It turned out that homework was a major problem every night. The boy would finish his assignments and then bring them to his father for checkout. That was the good news. The bad news was that if the work was not absolutely perfect, the father would tear it all up!

When asked how many times—on the average—the dad was tearing up the kid's homework, the mother said about three times per evening. No wonder the boy was getting demoralized.

I insisted on seeing the father. Dad blustered into the office insisting that his son was going to learn to do things right and that he was going to master his subjects, etc., etc. I replied that the boy was indeed learning a lot: he was learning to hate his father, to hate schoolwork, and to hate himself, and, if this nightly routine was continued, it would produce a high school dropout in four years. That was the end of that.

If the youngster's work is about 80 per cent neat, correct and complete, use the PNP procedure. You don't have to tell the child that it's perfect, just that it's good enough. Some perfectionists may squirm at this suggestion, but they should try to stay in touch with the emotional realities of childhood.

Charting

Charting lends itself very well to homework. Here's an easy system that can be used.

Since it's usually the older kids who have trouble with homework, a five-point scale can be used for them instead of stickers. Five is a high mark and one is a low mark. A child can earn one point for each of the following things:

Neat - 1 point
Correct - 1 point
Thorough - 1 point
No complaining - 1 point
Starting on his/her own - 1 point

The kids can get each of the first three points by doing better than whatever approximate percentage of neatness, correctness and completeness you have required. The last point is the crucial one: if you can get a child to start on his own, the battle is half won. You can set up friendly incentive games with this last point. For example, three days in a row of starting on your own at the proper time earns a bonus point. Or starting more than fifteen minutes early and finishing in a reasonable amount of time earns a bonus point. Put on your thinking cap and see what other schemes you can come up with.

Remember that for many kids with academic handicaps, you may very well have to use artificial reinforcers to help motivate the child over the homework hurdle.

Also, don't forget that kitchen timer. Sometimes it can be used to help break up the work into smaller, manageable pieces. If the child complains that the ticking bothers him (most don't), use some kind of sand hourglass or a quiet electric timer.

Practicing Obnoxious Musical Instruments

The tactics for getting kids to practice follow the same logic as those for homework. Avoid the same "don'ts" and try natural consequences first if the child is just starting out. The PNP method still applies—make sure any of your comments are started with positive reinforcement, then add the negative if it's absolutely necessary.

The spirit of the Rough Checkout also applies in the sense that 8:30 p.m. is no time for perfection. Charting also can help a lot. For some kids just putting on the chart the number of minutes they practiced can be enough to keep them going. For others, artificial reinforcers may be necessary, but remember that the points for no complaining and—especially—for starting on your own are very helpful.

Now that the homework and practicing are out of the way, it's time for bed!

18

Bedtime and Nighttime Waking

F or many parents, putting the kids to bed is a daily nightmare. In theory, bedtime may be nine o'clock, but at 10:30 the children are still wandering around the house, asking for drinks, or going to the bathroom for the twentieth time. This routine may be accompanied by a good deal of arguing and screaming, which only serves the purpose of making sure that everyone stays awake to watch the late movie together.

With a little thought, this kind of end to the evening can be avoided. Many of the Start behavior tactics can be used for bedtime. Put them together and you will have the Basic Bedtime Method (two-to-three-year-olds will need a little extra help).

Basic Bedtime Method

First and foremost, set a bedtime for the kids and stick to it as much as possible. The time may vary, of course, depending on whether it's a school night or a weekend, or whether it's during the school year or summertime. Let's assume that you have a nine-year-old, and you decide that nine o'clock will be the time to go to bed.

At 8:30 you set a timer for 30 minutes and tell the child that it's time to get ready for bed. This means that the youngster must do everything required to prepare for bed—on his own—and then report to you. (If the child is two or three, you'll have to help him get ready, but the same rewards/consequences apply.) If the child has in fact completed all the necessary tasks, you dish out a little Sloppy PVF. The time that is left between 8:30 and nine allows you to read a story or to simply sit and talk.

This approach serves three purposes. It is an immediate reinforcer for the child's doing a good job of getting ready for bed. It is also a good opportunity for you to spend a little quiet time together, which most kids value quite a bit. And finally, these moments with you help the kids relax and get more in the mood for going to sleep. You certainly wouldn't want them running around and yelling right before they're supposed to hit the sack.

If you have trouble coming up with the list of all that needs to be done, just think of all the things they usually tell you *they haven't done* after they are in bed, and you'll have it right away.

"I'm hungry."
"I'm scared."
"I need a drink."
"I have to go to the bathroom."
"These pajamas itch."
"There's a burglar in the basement."
"When's daddy coming home?"

Etc., etc., etc. Every item on their list should be taken care of *before* bedtime.

One caution here. Don't lie down on the bed. This has nothing to do with anything Freudian or sexual. It just so happens that there is a biological law that says: if you are over 25 years of age and it's past eight o'clock in the evening and you spend more than three minutes in a horizontal position, you're gone! The kids will love having you sleeping next to them, but they may get dependent on it and this goofs up their bedtime routine.

When nine o'clock rolls around, tuck the child in, kiss him goodnight, and leave the room. At this point some parents say, "How naive you are; the kid is right behind me!" What if he won't stay in bed?

Getting Out of Bed

Some kids just can't seem to stay in bed after you tuck them in. You put them down and they get up. You try to go about your business. They are always coming up with some new reason for getting out of bed.

What you should do about this problem is based on a basic principle: *if a child gets out of bed, the longer he is out of bed and/or the longer he stays up, the more reinforcement he gets.* The only conclusion, therefore, is that you have to cut him off at the pass. It is no fun, but this is no time for wishful thinking—or ridiculous conversations about why he should stay in bed. What you do is park yourself in a chair in the doorway to his bedroom. Get a good book if you want. Sit with your back to him and don't talk no matter what he says. If he gets out of bed and comes to you, take him gently by the arm or pick him up and put him back.

If you have a child who is a bit older (seven or over), you might be able to use charting to help the youngster stay in bed. Be careful with this tactic, however, because there is unique problem when it comes to bedtime. In general, rewards and punishments are most effective when they are given out immediately. Some studies have shown that even a few minutes delay in administering consequences can sometimes have a dramatic effect on their usefulness.

If you are using charting with bedtime, you cannot tell the child right away how he did. If he does really well, he won't be awake for you to talk to. Therefore, there must be quite a long delay before he finds out how you rated him (like the next morning), and you may find that this delay reduces the effectiveness of the procedure.

Nighttime Waking

Many children go through periods from time to time when they wake up at night. Some kids may get out of bed a dozen or more times, while others will just make noise or say something and then go back to sleep. Nighttime problems are among the hardest to handle, because in the middle of the night most parents aren't quite in their right minds—and neither are their kids. It's also very aggravating to be awakened from a sound sleep, and it can have a very bad effect on your next day at work.

Handling these situations incorrectly can make things worse very rapidly, and the number of times the kid wakes up can get more frequent and more traumatic for everybody. When people don't get enough sleep, their mood on the next day is affected, and by the time the next night rolls around, they're really cranked out of shape.

There are several guidelines that have proven to be very effective in modifying these nighttime episodes so the child gets back to sleeping through the night.

1. Accept some periodic waking as normal

Treat periodic waking as a temporary stage. This way of thinking will help you be less upset. Obviously, if the problem has been going on for the last four years, it's not a temporary "stage."

2. No Talking and No Emotion

These rules apply doubly for nighttime, because talking and emotion— especially anger—wake everyone up. Ever tried to sleep when you're furious? It doesn't work. Even asking the child what's wrong is most often useless, because he's groggy, not in his right mind, and can't tell you much. No Talking and No Emotion apply to fears and bad dreams, too; try to discuss them the next day if you can.

3. Assume the child may have to go to the bathroom

Even though they don't or can't say it, many kids are awakened by the urge to go. But they're so sleepy they aren't sure what the feeling is and can't verbalize. So try putting them on the toilet and see what happens. Don't ask them unless you know from vast experience they are capable of giving you an accurate answer.

4. Be gentle and quiet

Handle and guide the children softly as you stagger through the dark.

Don't grab or push them around and don't say anything. Bite your tongue, even though you may be irritated that they woke you up. Remember that you want them to remain sleepy and groggy.

5. No lights!

Lights wake you and the child up more. Your eyes should be dark-adapted in the middle of the night, so try to stagger around without turning anything on.

6. Don't go to the child's room unless you have to

When do you have to? If they are really screaming or if they come to you first. Some kids will make a little noise and then go back to sleep—give them a chance to do so.

7. Don't let the child sleep with you on a regular basis

Sleeping together can become a habit that's hard to break later. It may be the easiest way to quiet them down right at the time—and staying in bed certainly is tempting—but you will pay for these moments of weakness later. One exception: if there's a terrible storm going on outside, let the kids sleep on the floor next to your bed with sleeping bags and pillows. They'll do it. Otherwise, get them back in their room.

Now let's put these rules together and think through some possible sequences that might occur.

Mark, age 9

Mark has been sleeping regularly through the night. Tuesday night, however, he watches a rather scary movie on TV. At 2:45 a.m. you hear a few short, disconnected sentences.

Wait for a few minutes to see if he'll awaken or get up, but don't go to his room. After a few minutes he goes back to sleep and is peaceful for the rest of the night.

Jennie, age 6

Jennie has been restless in bed for a few nights, but hasn't gotten up. Thursday night, however, she appears at your bedside, shakes you by the arm a bit, and says she's scared.

Say nothing, but get up, put your arm around her shoulders, and steer her to the bathroom. Have her sit on the toilet for awhile, with no lights turned on. Then steer her gently back to bed, tuck her in, and give her a kiss. Wait for a second, see that she's falling asleep, then go back to bed.

Jim, age 4

Jim has been getting up several times a night. He won't go back to bed by himself and starts raising a ruckus if you tell him to go back. You can't tell if he's frightened or what. If you take him to his room, he cries or starts yelling when you try to leave. He says he wants to sleep with you. You know he's not sick, because he was just checked out by your pediatrician.

This situation is more difficult, obviously, than the first two examples. You don't want Jim to wake everyone in the house, but you don't like the idea of giving in to his testing either. What should you do?

When Jim appears at your bedside, escort him to the bathroom first—no lights, no talking, etc. Then take him to his room, put him in bed, and tuck him in. Now you know he'll cry if you try to leave, so before he gets a chance to do that, get a chair, park yourself by the bed, and wait till he goes back to sleep. This routine is not fun at all, but it works. If you've done the other things right—like no lights or arguing—your son should still be somewhat sleepy.

With some kids this procedure must be repeated several times a night for several weeks before they start sleeping through again. Our record so far for most times getting up in one night is 17! If you think you'll have to sit by the bed, get the chair ready beforehand. After a few nights, gradually start moving the chair out of the room, so you wind up sitting just outside the door where the child can't see you. If he asks if you're still there, make some noise like sniffing or moving around, but try not to talk. Soon after that, you shouldn't have to even sit in the chair.

Suzie, age 8

Suzie sleeps almost all the way through, but likes to get up at 5:30 a.m. and come to see you, ready to start her day. You've told her to go back to bed, but she won't.

There are several things you can try. First, consider adjusting her bedtime back an hour, say from eight to nine; she may not need that much sleep. Use the Basic Bedtime Method. Second, make sure her room isn't getting too much sunlight too early—that often wakes kids up.

Third, you can try the procedure from the third example. Put Suzie on the toilet, escort her to bed, and then see if she'll go back to sleep. If it's obvious that she won't, you will next try to train her to play in her room instead of waking you or someone else.

How do you do this? Try a combination of charting and the 1-2-3. Make a chart—using stars or numbers—that will keep a record of how well she does in the morning *playing by herself* and *not waking anyone*. She is to stay in her room if she's younger, but may go downstairs and watch TV if she's older or it's not ridiculously early in the morning. Give Suzie her score on the chart and some Sloppy PVF when you get up.

If she forgets and comes to you at 5:30, you say calmly, "Go back to bed, that's 1." Going back to bed at this point is a START behavior that takes less than two minutes. If she argues or doesn't go, you may count her out, and you may have to escort her back to her room. No extra talking and no emotion.

Physical pain can certainly wake kids up at night, so if they haven't had a physical lately and they start waking, it might be a good idea to have them checked out. In the meantime, use the procedures described here. Share the joy, if possible: if Mom and Dad are both available, take turns getting up. Sometimes it's fairly grueling, but it pays off in the end.

Questions

What if the youngster is not ready for bed and it's nine o'clock?

You can put him in bed with his clothes on. Take off his shoes so he's more comfortable. If he's just a little tyke (2 or 3), *you* put his pajamas on. And remember, don't get caught up in the tempting alternative of lecturing the child about what he should have done. It's late, you're tired, he's tired, and it's all too easy to slip up.

Someone told me that floor fans help kids sleep. What kind of sense does that make?

Believe it or not, floor fans do help some children go to sleep and stay asleep. Floor fans produce what is sometimes called "white noise," which is simply a monotonous, repetitive sound that is not disturbing. White noise tends to cover other night noises that may keep kids awake, such as a door closing, a car going by, a toilet flushing, a TV, etc. Some people also feel that the noise of a fan is in itself a kind of natural tranquilizer that encourages sleep.

Remember, though, it's the noise your looking for—not the wind—so don't blow the fan right on anybody. Actually, in the summer the air circulation can help too. White noise also makes it easier for you to sneak out of your son's or daughter's room at 3 a.m., after you've gotten up with the child for the second time!

19

The Family Meeting

W hen the kids are little, your house should be a dictatorship, and when they are 17 it should be almost, but not quite, a democracy. Obviously, the 1-2-3 is a tactic that doesn't give the kids much say in the discipline. That's the way it should be for the welfare of the children as well as the parents. You decide what is Stop behavior and you punish it with a brief time out, but you do so in a way that is fair, calm and not emotionally or physically abusive. Charting and other Start behavior tactics are friendlier, but they still are largely designed and applied by you.

Dictatorship to Democracy

Somewhere along the line, however, as the kids get older, you want to begin the evolution toward a more democratic way of conducting business around the house. A good time to start is when the kids are in the primary grades in school. Don't try this when the children are three or four years old, because it will probably just aggravate you and confuse them.

There are several reasons why the Family Meeting is a good idea. As the kids get older—and hopefully more rational—it is more appropriate that they have a bigger voice in the issues that affect them. Kids also will often cooperate better when they have a say in what's going on. And finally, children need this kind of training for a later time when they have their own families.

The Family Meeting is a good way to start giving the kids more of a voice in household operations. You can use it to discuss not only discipline, but also such communal issues as laundry, allowances, bedtimes, renting movies, vacations, food, fights, etc. The meetings will be more democratic, but you will still—if necessary—have the final say. You'll be doing more talking, but only at the meeting itself. The No-Talking rule will still apply when a rule is being enforced.

The Family Meeting can take place as often as you wish: once every week or two is ideal. You can also call special meetings whenever a unique or urgent problem comes up. Kids can request a meeting themselves.

How to Run the Meeting

The format of the meeting is very simple. Mom or Dad (not both at the same time) is the chairperson and has the responsibility for keeping order and staying on task. Older children can take a shot at running the meeting themselves from time to time. The chairperson sees to it that the agenda is followed and that each person gets a chance to speak without being interrupted.

Each person in the family can bring to the meeting a problem that he or she wants resolved. Then the chairperson guides the group through the following steps:

1. One person describes the problem he or she wants resolved.
2. Every other person gives their thoughts and feelings about that problem.
3. Next, the floor is opened for proposals for solutions; anyone can speak, but one at a time.
4. A solution is agreed upon to be tried out. It may combine different aspects of the suggestions from different people. If there are disagreements, Mom and Dad have the final say.
5. The agreed-upon solution is written down on a piece of paper

that is posted on the refrigerator, or it can be written in a Family Meeting journal, notebook or computer.

6. The next person brings up his or her problem, and steps 2-5 are repeated.

All solutions are considered experimental. If they don't work too well, they can always be reviewed at the next meeting. Proposals should be concrete, specific and practical, but don't be afraid to make them flexible and imaginative!

Sitting through these meetings is not always easy; it's a good idea to keep them under an hour so you don't go crazy. Many parents have agreed that the Family Meeting is one of the *most aggravating and effective* things you can do with your kids. It sounds contradictory, but if you can get through the process, people do have a greater tendency to follow through with the agreed-upon solutions. It's also nice that everyone has a chance to be heard and to learn some negotiation skills—an excellent preparation for marriage!

Examples

Case 1: Who's been drinking all the pop around here, anyway?

Sandy brings this weighty issue to the Family Meeting. She explains that Mom usually buys an eight-pack of soda, and there are four people in the family, but she's not getting her two bottles. There's never any left! The issue is discussed, with her brother, Mom and Dad throwing in their opinions. Then a solution is agreed upon.

When an eight-pack enters the house, all bottles will be initialed: two for Mom, two for Dad, two for Sandy, and two for brother. If you drink your two bottles, you're done. If you want another bottle, you have to check the eight-pack to see if there's a full bottle and, if so, whose initials are on it. If there is one, you may purchase it for 50 cents. If the person says no, no Badgering or Intimidation is allowed. This agreement is then posted on the refrigerator.

Case 2: When is bedtime during the summer?

The kids (10 and 12) have conspired to suggest at the meeting that summer bedtime should be different from during the school year. In fact, they don't think they should have a specific bedtime at all during the summer, since they can sleep the next day.

Mom and Dad, incredibly, agree to try the plan on one condition: if the parents go to bed before kids, the kids have to be amazingly quiet and cannot wake up Mom and Dad at all. Otherwise the deal will be changed.

20

Slipping

Nobody is perfect. Parents and teachers are human beings who have good days and bad days. Many people have used the 1-2-3 religiously for years and years, but for most of us it is often a struggle to stay consistent and to remember what we're supposed to be doing.

The problem we're talking about here is called "slipping." Some people call it backsliding. It means you start out well, get things shaped up, and then slip back into your previous ways of operating. The 1-2-3 switch sort of goes to the "Off" position. The old status quo has a nasty way of sneaking back up on us. Slipping can occur gradually over a period of months or years, or it can happen more suddenly.

Short-Term Slipping

In the course of a day it's easy to get distracted when there's always so much going on. You have to go to work, drive the kids all over the place, cook (or go get fast food), answer junk phone calls, help with homework, call your mother, try to find a little time to read the paper and so on. When you're trying to do nine things at once, who can remember the No-Talking and No-Emotion rules?

You can! It's not easy, but it beats arguing and screaming, which only add to your troubles, making you feel angry and guilty on top of everything else.

Let's imagine you have just gotten home at 5:30, after having had a hard day at work and picking up one child from soccer and another from piano. Now it's time to make dinner. The kids have been fighting like cats and dogs and you're starting to lose it:

> "He's hitting me!"
> "I was not! You're a pig!"
> "Shut up, you idiot!"
> "Knock it off, guys."
> "Pig."
> "Idiot."
> "Now you kids knock it off, YOU HEAR ME? I'm sick and
>   tired of the two of you picking at each other all the time."
> "Don't pinch me. DON'T! MOM, he's gonna..."
> "DIDN'T YOU GUYS COME WITH EARS?! What did I
>   just say?! That's it, no TV for either one of you tonight."
> "That's not fair. I wasn't doing anything." (Cries)
> "Ha, ha. You can't watch the moo-vee."
> "Neither can you, dummy."

What do you do in this situation? First, remember that you've forgotten the program. The sooner you catch yourself, obviously, the better. Then do a "mini-Kickoff," telling the kids you're going back to counting. Then shut up and count. In the situation above a time out could be worth 30 minutes off TV time or an earlier bedtime.

Let's take it from the top, with Mom or Dad making an effective—though belated—recovery:

> "He's hitting me!"
> "I was not! You're a pig!"
> "Shut up, you idiot!"
> "Knock it off, guys."
> "Pig."
> "Idiot."

"Now you kids knock it off, YOU HEAR ME? I'm sick and
tired of the two of you picking at each other all the time."
"Don't pinch me. DON'T! MOM, he's gonna..."
"OK, gang. I'm not doing my job right. We're going back to
counting. As of right now you both are on 1. You guys hit
three, it's 15 minutes off your TV time for tonight. It's up
to you."
"That's not fair. I wasn't doing anything." (Cries)
"Oh, yeah, little Miss Innocent."
"That's 2 for both of you."
(Silence. Both kids pout, but have nothing more to say.)

An NBA referee couldn't have done better.

Long-Term Slipping

You're doing fine with the 1-2-3 and charting, when Mom has to go into
the hospital for a week. Dad stays home and tries to control the chaos.
When Mom comes home—still in pain from the surgery—the kids are
nervous and acting like wildmen. You forget the charts and go back to
nagging, arguing and yelling.

The situation deteriorates further. About three weeks later, you wake
up in the middle of the night and wonder, "What happened to the 1-2-3?"

Some people stick to the straight and narrow forever, but that's not
typical. Most parents and teachers slip some. What causes slipping? The
most common causes are:

- Just plain time
- Visitors
- Illness
- Travel
- New babies

For the most part, any significant disruption of daily routine has the
potential to cause slipping.

What do you do? First of all, accept it as normal. Nobody's perfect,
including you, and you shouldn't expect yourself to be. Life's also a bit

more complex than any of us ever anticipated, especially when it comes to raising children.

Second, it's *back to basics*. Almost invariably, when parents come to me and say, "It's not working anymore," what is happening is:

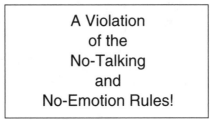

A Violation
of the
No-Talking
and
No-Emotion Rules!

This point cannot be emphasized strongly enough. So we go back and review the theory and the procedures very carefully, and then send Mom and Dad on their way. This brief refresher course usually takes care of the problem.

Fortunately, the Stop and Start behavior training methods described here are simple and can be resurrected and reapplied with little difficulty. The fact that you've used them once and slipped does not hurt their effectiveness the second time around.

Just go back to basics. Turn that 1-2-3 switch to "On."

Over the course of your kids' growing-up time, you may go through a number of slips and recoveries. Daily, monthly, even annually. That's normal. Each time you catch yourself slipping, just pick yourself up, take a deep breath, and go back to what you know works best.

Part V

The 1-2-3
in the Classroom

21

Counting for Teachers

Teachers have used the 1-2-3 successfully in the classroom for many years. In fact, in many preschool and grammar schools, the 1-2-3 is the basic discipline system for the entire school. What we have discussed so far is easily adapted to the classroom, where the 1-2-3 is employed in a manner that is very similar to its use at home.

Some schools use the 1-2-3 in the classroom, and have also trained many of their parents to adopt the method. This coordination is nice for the children, because they then have the same system in both places. The consistency makes it easier for them to respond appropriately. Like their parents and teachers, children are happier when there is less hassling about discipline.

This chapter will provide some general information about the application of the 1-2-3 in the school setting. There is room here, however, for a good deal of flexibility and creativity as the 1-2-3 is applied at different levels, so the following chapters will examine how the 1-2-3 can be used in preschool and daycare, in kindergarten through fifth grades, and in a junior high school setting (grades 6 through 8).

Discipline Before Learning

Some form of order in the classroom is required if anybody is going to learn anything. Many teachers feel, however, that their training either ignored or only touched on the matter of discipline. Discipline problems are often seen, therefore, as unexpected and unnecessary intrusions into the academic day, rather than as an inevitable—although unpleasant—part of the process of education.

Since there is often little preparation for managing children who have trouble following the rules, a teacher's struggle with this problem may often be a spontaneous reflection of his or her personality. On the one hand are teachers who have a natural ability to intimidate. Their innate manner communicates clearly that "you don't mess with me." On the other hand are teachers who feel uncomfortable with discipline, and in between are those who have achieved the "happy medium"—those who have the best qualities of each type. Each of these kinds of teacher has some good and some bad points, and may develop difficulties at different grade levels.

The instructor who is uncomfortable with discipline will have little problem with the children in the early grades, since the children there are usually quite anxious to please the teacher. Problem children—and their parents—may be difficult to handle, however. This teacher may have trouble setting and enforcing limits, especially with older kids, so in junior high or high school he or she may have an especially difficult time.

The more intimidating sort will also have no problem with the early grades, since the kids wouldn't dream of messing with her. However, this teacher may be tough on the self-esteem of the little ones without knowing it. She will be quite comfortable setting and enforcing limits, and will often be able to handle junior high and high school kids without suffering too much or hurting anyone else's self-esteem unduly. She may, however, run into battles with problem students and their parents.

Many teachers, of course, develop the happy medium on their own. They have very satisfactory ways of handling discipline without hurting children or being hurt themselves. They can enforce limits effectively, but also can be sensitive and understanding when necessary. For those who have the happy medium, the 1-2-3 can just make life easier.

However, for those who may be at one extreme or the other, the 1-

2-3 can help. For those uncomfortable with discipline, the 1-2-3 gives them a strategy—especially in higher grades. For those who may be too angry or intimidating, the 1-2-3 can help keep them under control, giving them a way of maintaining order without hurting anyone.

The 1-2-3 in the Classroom

Teachers can start using the 1-2-3 anytime, though it is a little easier to get going right from the beginning in September. Usually the teacher will do his version of the Kickoff conversation with the entire class. He then makes a list of "countable" offenses, sometimes in a class discussion where the kids help make the list themselves. It is still important to keep in mind the difference between Start and Stop behavior, because the tactics will be different. (We'll discuss teachers' Start behavior tactics later.)

After the method is discussed, the teacher needs to decide on a consequence for a student receiving a 3. For the preschoolers, kindergartners and kids through about the third grade, a time-out area—usually a chair, table or rug— is chosen. Most teachers like to, or are required to, keep the child in the room, rather than out in the hall. For fourth and fifth graders and junior high (6th grade to 8th grade) students, many—but not all—teachers feel a time out is no longer appropriate, and a consequence such as five or ten minutes subtracted from the student's recess or lunch, or some kind of after school "detention," may be substituted.

For the time-out procedure, an area in the back of the room or off to the side is often selected. Some teachers prefer to have the area blocked off visually from the rest of the class by something like a bookcase or file cabinet. A chair or desk can be put in the time-out area. If there are two chairs, they shouldn't be too close together and, if possible, should have something between them. There are usually no other materials available, though some teachers will allow children to do schoolwork during the rest period.

When a youngster is acting up, the teacher holds up one finger and says, "John, that's 1." This can be done in front of the class if it's done properly, because the intent is not to embarrass the child. Some embarrassment may be inevitable, but that's not bad. Think back to the idea mentioned before: if you don't want to be embarrassed, you can behave. Some teachers get so efficient at counting that they only have to make eye contact with the child and then hold up the appropriate number of fingers. This technique is often referred to as the "silent finger" approach.

When a child hits 3, he is instructed to go to the time-out area. Many teachers simply use a five-minute rest period (two or three minutes for the preschoolers), rather than the one-minute-per-year rule. Refusing to go to time out is treated as a major offense, and can be dealt with by a visit to (or from) the principal, a call to the parents, or a restriction of usual school privileges, such as recess or lunch or even the right to go home at 3:15 (detention). Goofing around too much during time out can be handled in a similar fashion. Teachers should tailor the consequences to the child and keep in mind that the more immediate the consequence, the more effective it is.

In some schools, time outs for more serious offenses (or the second or third time out in the same day) are served in the principal's office, but *without* a discussion with the principal. The child simply reports to the office and says he is there for a time out. No one is allowed to talk to him in either a friendly or a reprimanding way. After the required minutes, the student returns to the class.

Like parents, teachers need to keep in mind that kids are not little adults. It is probably true that most adults, when disciplining children, have a tendency to talk and explain things too much. Keep in mind that this extra verbiage is not merely an unfortunate habit. It is very destructive, because it elicits more testing and manipulation, and—even worse—it tends to place the responsibility for the child's good behavior more on the teacher than on the child. Then we have a situation that is more like, "I'll be good if you can talk me into it."

Behavioral Accounting

Teachers have unique problems that parents don't have. No parent, as far as we know, has to discipline 25 kids at home! A teacher must keep an eye on an entire class and also keep track of which kids are at which counts.

The job is not as daunting as it first appears, however. In a regular classroom on an average day, most children will not be counted at all. In a typical class of 25 students, it is unusual if more than three or four kids receive a count of any kind, and on many—or even most—days no one will receive a time out.

Still, some kind of record keeping is necessary and several options are available. Some teachers use the old blackboard routine. With the first count, the child's name goes on the board. The second and third counts result in checkmarks after the name. If the child goes to 3, the time out is served and the name can be erased. Many teachers feel, however, that the name on the board is too much like "rubbing it in." In addition, sometimes the names do not get erased when they are supposed to, causing unfair embarrassment the next day.

One teacher came up with a more creative idea. She made a big stoplight (approximately 24 inches by 6 inches) out of cardboard, with the usual red light on top, yellow in the middle, and green on the bottom. This was then laminated, with a strip of black vinyl hung from the bottom. Attached to the vinyl were clothespins, and on each clothespin was the name of a child.

If a child received a count, he had to get up and move his clothespin from the vinyl to the green light, which stood for a count of 1. The same procedure was followed for a 2 count (clothespin on the yellow light), and finally, if the child hit 3, the clothespin was put on the red light while the time out was served. Upon leaving the time-out area, the youngster was then allowed to put his name back on the black vinyl strip.

The advantage of this setup is that at any one time you can simply glance at the stoplight and see where every student in the class is. On the other hand, the names are not as large and obvious as they are when written on the board. Other setups using big, colored numbers or colored containers (with names on popsicle sticks) can work equally well.

Even with these methods, some teachers feel that less notoriety is better with any behavioral accounting procedure, especially when dealing with children in the higher grades. One easy method involves the teacher merely writing the student's name on a small note pad when giving the first count or warning. Further counts are then marked after the name.

Since few kids normally get counted in the first place, some teachers just keep the counts in their heads. This tactic shouldn't be used, though, unless it can be done accurately. Keep in mind that many children also keep track—both for themselves as well as for their classmates—and they may try to correct a teacher who is at the wrong number.

Many teachers rightly feel that the 20-minute rule needs to be modified for the classroom. In other words, they feel that allowing up to three offenses in a 20-minute period, and then going back to a count of zero, makes for too much possible misbehavior. Some teachers, therefore, extend the time during which the counting to 3 continues. Some extend the time so it coincides with a usual class period (45-50 minutes or so) in the school day. Others have been more strict and have extended it to the entire morning, with the children then starting again at a count of zero after lunch. In general, most teachers feel that holding the counts over longer periods is more appropriate for older children.

If 1-2-3 Doesn't Solve the Problem

If a child responds to the 1-2-3, but her frequency of problem behaviors stays at an unsatisfactory level, other steps need to be considered. Occasionally, something as simple as moving her seat or some other educational adjustment may help, but often a more extensive look at what is going on becomes necessary.

Some schools use the following sequence:

1. Classroom adjustments (e.g., move seat)
2. Parent conference with teacher (child participates in part of the conference)
3. Parent conference with principal (or assistant principal); restriction of participation in school activities may be considered
4. Social worker or behavioral consultant involved
5. Special services team involved
6. Case study (if not previously done)

These interventions attempt to find out if something else is going on that is causing the child's problem, such as a learning disability, Attention Deficit Disorder, family problems or other psychological diagnosis (e.g., depression or anxiety).

Classroom Benefits

Over the years teachers have identified a number of important benefits—both for themselves and for their students—that occur as a result of using the 1-2-3:

Clear and Simple

Teachers feel the 1-2-3 is easy to learn and easy to understand for everyone involved: children, teacher and parents. Having the rules and disciplinary procedures perfectly clear makes for more order in the classroom. Children respond better when they know exactly what the consequences will be.

Instruction Time Not Wasted

The counting method is crisp and simple enough so that, when done properly, it doesn't waste the valuable and limited time available for learning. Giving a count or warning is done without a lot of chatter, persuasion or arguing. It doesn't have to embarrass or aggravate a youngster and thus provoke a counterattack.

Teacher Not Exhausted by Discipline

What about discipline can exhaust a teacher? One problem is the useless verbal hassles that occur when a teacher falls back into the "little adult" assumption. This regression can lead to the nagging and lecturing that tend to produce the "Talk-Persuade-Argue-Yell" routine (teachers don't usually hit). That's tiring.

A second energy-sapping problem develops when a teacher becomes so involved arguing with one student that the rest of the class goes bananas in a kind of chain reaction. Now the entire class has to be brought under control.

Discipline with Dignity

As one teacher put it, "The 1-2-3 allows us to achieve discipline that maintains the dignity of the students." Misbehavior is handled routinely, and is not treated as if it were the worst thing in the world or some kind of personal insult. The No-Talking and No-Emotion rules see to it that children feel a minimum of "put-down" when they are disciplined.

No Attention for Misbehavior

Some children who have been having problems for a while seem to enjoy causing trouble and being the center of attention. A teacher who talks too much and gets too upset plays right into their hands and actually reinforces the disruptive behavior. The 1-2-3—done properly—does not give undue attention to the wrong things.

Testing and Manipulation Identified

We now know the tricks the kids can pull when they are frustrated. The Six Kinds of T&M have been discovered! Life will never be the same for the difficult youngsters who wish to successfully pull off a dose or two of Badgering, Threat or Martyrdom. Teachers find it is very helpful to identify to themselves—right when it is occurring—the kind of testing that is going on. This problematic behavior can then be taken less seriously and also managed more effectively.

Do kids test teachers differently than they test their parents? Generally the six types of T&M are the same, but teachers who are also parents of two-to-twelve-year-olds often say that in school they get less Intimidation, Threat, and Physical tactics, but more Butter Up. Martyrdom seems to be a favorite in both locations.

On the Playground

Free time and free play outside are occasions when kids can get into all kinds of hassles. Energy and activity levels are high and there is little structure. Fortunately, children also value their free time a lot, which makes the 1-2-3 very easy to use for playground supervisors.

If a child is engaging in some kind of Stop behavior, he is given a 1. Because of all the noise, the warning may have to be shouted. That's OK as long as the volume is not an expression of anger. If the child hits 3, he must spend five minutes sitting next to the teacher or monitor, watching the others play. Kids hate that, so they will work hard not to get counted.

Some teachers like to try something else when two kids are arguing or fighting. The children are first interrupted. Then they are instructed that they must work out their difference themselves. If they succeed in doing this, both kids receive some positive feedback. If this strategy doesn't work, the children will then be counted.

Parents and Homework

Teachers are often in the position of having to encourage parents to encourage their children to do their homework. If you suggest to parents that they "get after" their kids about homework, be sure to offer some specific methods. Those described in Chapter 17, which include Sloppy PVF, Timers and Charting, as well as the "Positive-Negative-Positive" method and the "Rough Checkout," are good examples.

Otherwise, what Mom and Dad may do spontaneously—nagging, yelling or interrupting the child in the middle of her favorite TV program—may be counterproductive.

Start Behavior

Start behavior strategies were discussed in Chapter 14. They can all be helpful for teachers, especially Sloppy PVF (positive reinforcement), Kitchen Timers and Charting. The Docking System can be used sometimes if the class is on a "token economy" type of reward system, but it has more limited application in the classroom, since a teacher is not going to do a child's work for her.

The next chapters will describe how the 1-2-3 has been used in real-life school settings. The descriptions combine some of the best ideas from a number of different educators.

You'll discover there is not necessarily one right way to apply the 1-2-3. In some schools, for example, all teachers are required to use it. In other schools some do and others don't. In some preschools and kindergartens, the 1-2-3 is used right off the bat in the beginning of the year, while in others it is used as a "backup" system with extremely difficult classes or difficult students.

You'll also find that the 1-2-3 is only a part of a teacher's behavior-management skills. There is much more to running a classroom, and teachers have time and again demonstrated their ingenuity and creativity in coming up with an overall program that includes—and goes beyond—what is covered in this book.

22

Preschool and Daycare

C hildren in preschool and daycare situations—approximately ages two to five—are at the stage where they need to learn basic socialization skills as well as the ability to follow the instructions involved in a daily routine. Parents want their children in these situations to be able to respect the rights of others, to learn to give and take, and to begin to feel good about themselves. They also want their kids to be able to handle a time period of two and one-half hours or more that involves activities such as music, story time, snack time, free play, group sharing time and arts and crafts.

Obviously, good, consistent discipline provides a basis for allowing these kinds of learning to occur. If a class of children—no matter how small—is continually out of control and no one gets along, little learning occurs and everyone's self-esteem suffers.

Before Using the 1-2-3

Here's one way of handling discipline at this level. Since these children are just learning how to socialize and handle routines, it may not be necessary to start right out with the 1-2-3 (though many schools do). Some preschool or daycare teachers also feel they want to avoid, in the beginning, singling out the child by the counting process. If a child is out-of-line with his behavior in a group, the teacher's first two alternatives can be:

1. Simple distraction: guide or interest the child in another activity
2. Separation from the group for a short time

Little kids are fairly easy to distract, and then the whole problem can be forgotten. If the child needs to be separated from the group, he can sit in a chair or a spot on a rug for a kind of time-out period. In some preschools, the child is then allowed to determine when he wishes to cooperate and is ready to return to the group. If problems continue, however, for subsequent rest periods, the teacher determines when the child will return.

Meeting with Parents

With the methods described above, most kids eventually learn to follow the rules and the routines. If problems continue beyond this point, then the 1-2-3 will come into play. The teacher and school directors meet with the parents and discuss the child's behavior at school. Teachers also ask about the child's behavior at home, since there are often marked similarities in how children behave at home and at school. They also inquire about the kind of discipline the parents use and how the child responds to it.

The idea of this meeting is not only to identify problems, but also to propose solutions. So after this initial orientation, the *1-2-3 Magic* program is explained to the parents, and the preschool staff emphasize to the parents that the method works especially well if it can be done at both home and school. Parents' responses to this suggestion are usually fairly positive, since they very likely have also been bewildered by the child's problem behaviors.

Initially in the discussions with parents, emphasis is placed on the No-Talking and No-Emotion rules, on the difference between Start and Stop behaviors, and on being consistent. Parents are required to read the *1-2-3 Magic* book or watch the video, and then they are asked to focus first on Stop behaviors. Teachers explain that Stop behaviors are those that interfere most with the child's ability to socialize, because they cause classmates to shy away from the child. They also explain that—in addition to counting obnoxious behavior—teachers at preschool and the parents at home should also consistently praise any positive behavior the child produces.

Many preschools also tell parents that the school will handle the child's behavior during the day, and that the child should not be held responsible again by the parents at home. In other words, no "double jeopardy." The child would have already received the consequences at school, and the difficult behavior should then be forgotten.

After the parents have read the *1-2-3 Magic* book, a second meeting is held to discuss questions about the program and when it will start. Then the game plan is twofold.

First, parents briefly do the Kickoff conversation (see Chapter 9) at home with the child (or all the children ages 2 to 12) and then get started—preferably on a weekend.

Second, the preschool teacher talks to the child individually at school and then begins the program at school that same week.

At school the child may be the only one in the class on the 1-2-3 system. When a time out is necessary, a time-out chair or rug in the room is used, rather than the child leaving the room. The only time a child will be removed from the room is if he is throwing a temper tantrum that is upsetting the other kids (see explanation below).

After a few weeks, parents (it is important to try to keep Dad involved) and teachers meet again to discuss how the program is going and any bugs in the system. Most schools feel they have great success when the 1-2-3 is implemented properly and consistently both at home and at school.

Other issues discussed in follow-up meetings can include who is responsible for counting (parent or teacher) during the brief period when the child arrives or leaves, or how to train sitters and others who watch the children to use the 1-2-3.

Temper Tantrums

Some kids have a harder time than others at this age in adjusting to new routines, and react with tantrums when frustrated (see testing tactic #2,

Intimidation, in Chapter 10). These outbursts can be handled in the following way. If the tantrum isn't too horrible in the classroom, it can be ignored, and attempts by the child to rejoin the group or activity can be reinforced.

If the tantrum is disturbing other children, the child will have to be removed. He is taken to the rest room (or other unoccupied and confined area with limited distractions), where two teachers or staff stay with the him until the tantrum is over. As the child is yelling or thrashing around on the floor or whatever, one adult periodically tells him—in a calm and reassuring voice—that he has two choices. He can either continue screaming on the floor and stay in the rest room with the teachers, or he can stop the tantrum and return to the classroom to play with friends. Nothing else is said. Patience is essential!

Of course, many preschools and daycare settings prefer to use the 1-2-3 right from the beginning with all the children. After only a brief orientation, youngsters at this age seem to get the idea more from experiencing the procedure. They make remarkable gains in maturity over the course of the year.

Preschool teachers have had very good success with *1-2-3 Magic* when it is applied as described here. They feel that the 1-2-3 helps reinforce the notion that the behavior—not the child—is unacceptable. In addition, the method does not lavish attention on negative behavior. Problem behavior is simply counted in a matter-of-fact way, allowing the teacher to spend a minimum amount of time on a difficult child. This, in turn, helps the other children remain positive about that child, rather than starting to avoid him during play.

23

Elementary Grades (K-5)

N ow we're getting more serious. Not only must children in these years master handling routines, following instructions and getting along with others, but they also are expected to actually learn something. Numbers, letters and other signs of academia start creeping in, and the school day is not quite as much fun as it was in preschool. As the years progress, the daily demands to sit still and pay attention to more and more difficult tasks increase dramatically. If class discipline is weak and behavior is out-of-line, these new skills will be more difficult to acquire.

Kindergarten

Kindergarten is kind of an "in between" year. The day is still short and the children are still allowed to move around a lot. On the other hand, kindergartners frequently are expected, by year end, to recognize and to write their ABCs, to be able to count to 100, to recognize and write the numbers up to about 20 or so, and to be able to recognize a few short words.

Kindergartners are also very sensitive at this age, their feelings can be easily hurt, and they see the teacher as a kind of god. Many have learned a lot about handling the demands of a daily routine in preschool, which makes the discipline task easier in general for many teachers.

Teachers' personalities and skills vary considerably, however. Some have a quality about them that automatically communicates, "you don't fool around in here," while others appear more anxious and less intimidating. Classes also vary more than the law of averages would seem to dictate. Some years the kids are a breeze to teach, and then there are the "classes from hell" that everyone dreads getting.

For kindergarten, it all boils down to this: some teachers will lean more toward the preschool methods described in the last chapter, where the 1-2-3 is used more as a backup method that kicks in only with more difficult children. Other kindergarten teachers, however, who may not naturally be intimidating or who may be dealing with a very difficult class, may prefer the 1-2-3 method described below for the primary grades.

Getting the Year Started

It will usually take two weeks or less to get the kids oriented to the 1-2-3 discipline system. For new kids in any grade, kindergartners and first graders, it is important to go over the procedures daily for the first two weeks. If children are second or third graders, of course, and they've been doing the 1-2-3 for the last year or two, it will be easier for them.

When a complete orientation is required, the teacher should explain the program in detail each day during the first week. During the second week, class discussions are geared toward the *children telling the teacher* how the system works. This exercise helps the teacher know how well the class understands the 1-2-3 and which kids may be having trouble grasping the concept.

Other methods that have been used to orient children to the 1-2-3 include showing part of the *1-2-3 Magic* video. One of the best segments is the "Twinkie example," showing the little girl testing her mother in the kitchen. Some teachers have also used role playing. After explaining the 1-2-3 and also describing the different kinds of Testing and Manipulation, the teacher selects students to demonstrate the different testing tactics. The teacher—or a student playing the teacher—then counts them.

Parents are oriented primarily in two ways. On the first day of school a note is sent home describing the discipline program and the classroom rules. This note is to be signed (preferably by both parents) and returned. This process helps to make sure that the parents understand the system and that they have agreed to it, and is also very helpful at a later date if a conference is required about behavioral problems.

The second part of parent orientation is a parent night, which should be held not later than the second week of school. As part of this program, the discipline procedures are again explained to the parents, and comments and questions are encouraged. Usually the *1-2-3 Magic* book and video are shown as references at the parent night, and parents are encouraged to borrow them to familiarize themselves with the program. Parents are told very clearly that it is in the children's best interests that the 1-2-3 be used both at school and at home.

Using the 1-2-3

Four or five important classroom rules, such as "Follow Directions," "Be a Friend," and "Listen Carefully" can be posted on the wall in the classroom. During the first two weeks the teacher will have explained what these rules mean and what will be counted. Common behaviors counted at this age include getting out of your seat, forgetting to raise your hand, arguing or fighting with someone, pushing in line, talking at the wrong time, and tattling.

Many teachers will also count "attitude." This can include excessive expressions (verbal or nonverbal) of disrespect or excessive pouting (see Chapter 8, Variations).

The teacher has explained that if a rule is broken, the child will be given the first warning, "That's 1." If the class is using the stoplight, the student must move his clothespin from below the stoplight and put it on green, or 1 (see description of stoplight in Chapter 21). A second incident will bring a 2; the child moves the clothespin again (to yellow). Kids are usually embarrassed having to get up to move the clothespin, which in itself acts as a deterrent to further misbehavior.

The third occurrence of a problem receives a "That's 3, take 5" from the teacher. Nothing else is said. The child moves his marker to 3 (red). He then serves a five-minute time out on a "time-out rug" that is located off to one side of the classroom. Five minutes is a good length of time for kids this age, rather than exactly one minute per year of their age. The little ones who do not tell time yet are instructed to just pay attention to the movement of the big hand on the clock. They are responsible for telling when the time out is up, moving their marker back down, and returning to their seat.

For children this age, getting a time out is a big deal. Many little children will become teary if they are counted at all, but especially if they are counted to 3. Some of this is simply due to embarrassment, which is not bad or harmful. It is part of how kids learn and is par for the course. The teacher should ignore the tears. The stoplight on the wall also gives a constant reminder of where everybody stands.

For the purposes of the 1-2-3, the school day is divided into two parts, morning and afternoon. For the kindergartners, of course, there is just one part, morning or afternoon. Warnings can add up to three during the entire morning (or afternoon), but at lunchtime everyone returns to zero and starts fresh. For example, a child might get a 1 at 9:30 a.m., a 2 at 11 a.m., and a 3 at 11:40 a.m.

Kids like the idea of starting fresh in the morning each day, and starting over each afternoon. Keep in mind, however, that in a typical class most kids will probably not be counted at all on an average day. On a typical day fewer than 20 percent of the children will receive a count at all, and fewer than that, of course, will receive a time out.

Counting can also be done in special classes, such as music, art, gym, library and computers. Those counts are usually kept separately from the regular classroom discipline program due to the difficulty involved in communicating this information to the main classroom teacher.

For Bigger Trouble

For children who do have more trouble keeping themselves in line, the following procedures can be used:

1st time out: lose sticker
2nd time out: note or phone call to parents
3rd time out: meeting with parents, principal and teacher

Stickers can be used as part of a charting system. For example, each child can earn a sticker by going the whole day without getting a time out. At the end of the day, the kids put their stickers on the chart. The chart is placed on a wall, bulletin board, fire escape door or whatever. Each child has a place on the chart—a brightly colored leaf, pumpkin, bucket or some other object—where he puts his sticker.

As it is at home, kids up to the ages of eight or nine like the daily stickers, which help reinforce good behavior at the end of each day. The stickers can also tie into a class reward. In the beginning of each calendar month, the class decides what reward or treat it would like to work for. It might be something like 20 minutes free time, a video, a pizza party at lunch, making ice cream sundaes, and so on. The reward takes place on the first day of the next month—if it is earned.

The teacher explains that to earn the reward, every child in the class must get at least 15 stickers for the month. The average month has slightly more than 20 school days, so this system does not require perfection. This room for error is important to children who do have more difficulty controlling themselves.

These children who have more behavioral difficulties will get some heat from other class members to stay in line or shape up. Reprimands from classmates, such as "Joey, you're gonna lose our treat," may be heard from time to time. These comments may be met with defiance or pouting, but they usually do help their receiver to self-control. Occasionally, the classroom teacher may need to count the reprimanders if they are becoming too self-righteous and nagging.

Counting the Whole Class

There are those days in a teacher's life when everybody seems to be going nuts at the same time. Everyone—kids and staff—seems to be more flaky during the days right before a vacation or near the end of the school year. And then there are some classes that are just more difficult in the first place.

At times, therefore, it may be helpful to count the entire class. The teacher says, "Class, that's 1 for everyone," or "If this doesn't stop, I'm going to have to count the whole class." After giving a count, of course, the teacher says nothing and stands quietly watching the class. What if the class hits 3? There's not enough room on the rug for 25 bodies, so one alternative is to simply have the children put their heads down on their desks for five minutes. This helps calm them down anyway. Then the teacher states when the time out is up, and the class continues with its discussion or next activity.

Counting the entire class can be tied into the class reward if necessary. For example, the third time in any one month that the whole class is timed out cancels the treat. Watch out if the prize is lost early in the month!

Two problems with counting the whole class should be kept in mind. First of all, many teachers use this tactic only as a last resort, since it sometimes makes everyone feel bad. Second, inevitably there are children who are not really misbehaving who will get counted along with the class; they will feel this procedure is unfair, but class time outs are not usually counted on an individual student's record.

Start Behavior Tactics

The main Start behavior strategies used in the classroom include Sloppy PVF, timers and charting.

Sloppy PVF (positive verbal feedback) is very important to little children and can have a big impact on their behavior. Teachers are often both very aware of this fact and also very good at praising their young charges on a regular basis, so we don't need to elaborate here a lot. A few points might be helpful, however.

In Chapter 14, we explained that praise should be tailored to the child. Some kids like it "syrupy" and some kids go more for the business-like kind. The rule here is: tailoring is more and more of a consideration the older the kids get. The little ones in kindergarten and first grade usually do fine with the more effusive reinforcement.

Praise can be directed not only toward individual kids, but also at the whole class or at separate work groups or teams. The praise should be very specific. "The red table is really working hard today. Everyone has their pencil in their hand, their eyes on their papers, and they're working quietly."

With the younger children, "next-door" or "across-the-room" praise can often be used to help a child who is off-task or misbehaving. Imagine Jimmy is staring out the window when he's supposed to be writing his numbers to ten. Right next to him, Sarah is working diligently. Out loud in front of the class teacher says, "I'm really impressed with how hard Sarah is working. Her pencil is in her hand and she's writing very neatly." Jimmy is reminded of the task without being embarrassed.

A teacher should always have a supply of a few kitchen timers. For people who don't like the ticking, hourglasses can be found in sand, liquid or LCD versions. Timers can be used from time to time for students who tend to daydream instead of work. They can be used to motivate clean-up times or other occasions when the whole class must get ready for something. They can also be used to time time outs.

Charting is always a friendly way of motivating the children to do what they're supposed to, and classrooms often have a number of charts on the wall. The little children like stickers that are colorful and interesting, and older kids are also interested in something that keeps a detailed record of their performance (like a gradebook!).

The only problem with charting in the classroom is that it takes time. If at the end of the day, for example, all children who had no time outs get to put their sticker on their chart, class time is used up. The teacher must feel that this is a useful activity and set aside the time accordingly. One group or row of children can go up at one time. Just as at home, it is important to keep up with the charting (the kids usually help with frequent reminders). Even then, the charts may need to be varied every few months so the children stay interested in them.

Benefits and Problems

Teachers have found that having a kind and fairly aggressive system of discipline such as *1-2-3 Magic* is a tremendous help in maintaining order in the classroom. Most children also seem to like the 1-2-3 program. Children encountering special difficulties such as Attention Deficit Disorder, learning disabilities or even temporary family crises also find it gives them something concrete and consistent to relate to.

Teachers have also commented that they like the idea of the two warning counts, rather than an immediate punishment. This technique gives the children a chance to shape up—and to be rewarded for that. Many teachers also feel the 1-2-3 helps them control *themselves*—giving them something concrete to do and preventing them from getting unnecessarily angry or upset.

As parents have found at home, though, the 1-2-3 only works well if it is done consistently. Being human, many people find themselves reminding the kids about a rule rather than first counting. "Julie, the rule is you must raise your hand first." This is not a big problem. What is a big problem, however, is giving the same child a second reminder instead of counting. Second and third reminders will encourage misbehavior and talking, and will waste class time.

Some teachers have also found that parent pressure affects their use of the 1-2-3. Some overly aggressive parents seem to feel that their child can do no wrong. The child pouts and gets teary when counted, tells the parents, and they then question the teacher about her methods. The teacher feels intimidated and starts reminding the child more, instead of counting. She also lets the child hold at 2 when a count of 3 really is warranted. Over a period of time—and not too long at that—this child's behavior will almost certainly deteriorate.

24

Junior High (Grades 6-8)

In grades six through eight—often called junior high—the going gets tougher for the teacher. The kids have long since ceased to see the teacher as some kind of god who can do no wrong. They are also feeling the first stirrings of you know what—adolescence! And in our society today, it certainly seems that adolescence comes earlier and earlier.

Welcome to Adolescence!

Adolescence means the kids want to be—or at least want to look like they are—more independent from their teachers and parents. They are also starting to identify more with their peer group than with adults or family, and in grades six through eight they are more and more experiencing the great teenage need to be different. That means different from you the adult, not necessarily from each other (adults don't usually wear baseball caps backwards or pierce three or four different body parts).

Adolescence is probably the time in life when a person's social sensitivity is at its highest. Adolescents, therefore, do not take well to being humiliated in public. For this reason, many will not act up in a classroom in the first place. Others, however, may be willing to take on a teacher in front of the class if they feel they are being embarrassed. Their feeling is "I will not lose to you" or "I will not let you make me look like an idiot with all my peers watching." This attitude gets even stronger if the student feels—rightly or wrongly—that a teacher's discipline is unfair or that it represents the teacher's simply grinding an axe at the student's expense.

Compounding the problem is this: in many junior highs each student has six or seven teachers during the day, each for a period of about 50 minutes. Many teachers feel that the combination of more teachers per day and incipient adolescence can make for more acting out in class. Team teaching may help, but it is still harder for any one teacher to keep track of the behavior and academic skills of so many students.

Whatever a teacher does with regard to discipline, it is likely that many students at this level will feel her actions are stupid. A natural part of adolescent psychology is the automatic tendency to question the methods of adults. And after all, what can you reasonably expect adolescents to say about a discipline system of any kind?

Classroom order must still be maintained, however, and some way of keeping track of misbehavior is necessary. Teachers have some difference of opinion about using the basic 1-2-3 procedure in grades six through eight. Some teachers have done it pretty much the same way as it is done in the primary grades. They hold up one finger and say "That's 1" for a warning, and at 3 the student takes a time out in a time-out area. One teacher had the youngster actually sit on the floor in the doorway to the room.

Other teachers, however, feel that holding up one finger and saying "That's 1" is too "juvenile" or too much of a "put-down" for kids this age. As a matter of fact, in some ways we agree—that's part of the reason why the 1-2-3 system is recommended for use with kids up to around age 12 (approximately sixth-grade age), and the *Surviving Your Adolescents* program is used after that.

It may also be true that—even with junior high kids—the perception of a "put down" in any discipline may have more to do with the way something is said, rather than the actual words. When the 1-2-3 is done properly, with no extra verbiage and no unnecessary emotion, it is not in any way an attempt to humiliate. That does not always mean, of course, that it will be perceived that way.

What to Do

What it boils down to, then, is this: some junior high teachers will be able to do the 1-2-3 just as it is done in the earlier grades. These will probably be the teachers who are very comfortable setting and enforcing limits, who do a minimum of talking about discipline, and who do not upset easily or act as though discipline were a form of revenge.

Other teachers may do best to modify several aspects of the program: the "silent finger" routine, the language and the consequence. Instead of holding up one finger or two fingers when giving a warning, the warnings are simply given verbally. This must be done efficiently, however, because it temporarily breaks the flow of whatever else the teacher is saying.

Second, the language of the warning can be changed, though it should still include the 1-2-3 concept; i.e., the third time you do something disruptive or out of line, there will be a consequence. Possible warnings might include:

> "John, I'm going to have to give you your first warning."
> "This is the first time I'm going to ask you to stop."
> "This is your second reminder."
> "We're on the second time now, Sue."
> "That's the third one, Matt."
> "I'm afraid that's strike three, Julie."

Third, the consequence that occurs with the third incident can be modified. Possibilities at the equivalent of 3 include a visit to the assistant principal, a reduction of free time (e.g., lunch) or other daily enjoyable activities (a kind of time out served in the office), or a detention (time served at the end of the school day).

Some of these consequences are delayed, of course, but they may not lose their impact because the kids are older and more able to associate the offense with the consequence. I cannot emphasize enough, however, that the power of any deterrent will be minimized if it is presented with excessive anger or an attitude of vengefulness. Adolescents will quickly sense that a "game" is in the air, and many will then play it with gusto. This reaction is not only very disruptive for the entire class, but it is also very discouraging and exhausting for the instructor.

Keeping Track

When a student has five to seven different teachers and the consequences involve something that has taken place at a different time and outside the classroom, recordkeeping becomes a necessary evil. Teachers must also coordinate with the main office regarding exactly what a student has done and what consequence he is subject to.

Any record keeping must be as simple and clear as possible, because it will be time-consuming. Computers and database software programs available today can help greatly with this process, but it still requires considerable staff time.

Two ideas can be helpful here: a "Behavioral Accounting Form" (or discipline slip) and a "Behavioral Accounting (or "Step") System." The Behavioral Accounting Form can be used by the classroom teacher for two purposes: to keep track of which student is at which point and to inform the office of what has happened. It needs to be brief, so that filling it out does not disrupt class time unnecessarily.

Here's one possibility. The teacher fills in what the student did that generated each warning, such as talking, being out of one's seat, bothering someone else, etc. This is done right in class and right after the action occurred, but it is done in a calm, unobtrusive and unchallenging manner. The "Third Occurrence" is no longer a warning since it nets the consequence. If the student is to report to the office, she takes the slip with her to give to the assistant principal.

The form might look something like this:

Behavioral Accounting Form

Date:...........................

Student's Name:..

1st Warning: _____

2nd Warning: _____

3rd Occurrence: _____

Teacher Signature:..

The Behavioral Accounting System is kept by the main office and provides an orderly way for keeping track of the disciplinary history of each student. Incidents that occur represent "steps" on a progressive discipline and intervention program. It is important to keep in mind here that the purpose of such a system is evaluative and corrective, not primarily punitive. Any student who is continually running into trouble needs to be disciplined, but her life may also need to be examined more closely to try to determine what is going wrong.

The Behavioral Accounting or Step System provides for both discipline and evaluation. Each time an incident occurs, the student "progresses" to another defined point on the system, which serves the purpose of being a consequence (inevitably unpleasant). Each point, however, also defines an evaluation and planning function. Information is gathered about what might be happening to cause the trouble and an attempt is made to make plans to eliminate the problems. A student can progress slowly (one step at a time) by accumulating "minor" infractions (e.g., tardies, referrals from class), or quickly (to the next "major" step) by engaging in more serious activities (e.g., fighting, smoking in school, etc.). A student can also receive an automatic 3 in class (skipping 1 and 2) and a "major" referral by doing something that the teacher considers to be very serious in the first place.

Here's what the Behavioral Accounting System might look like:

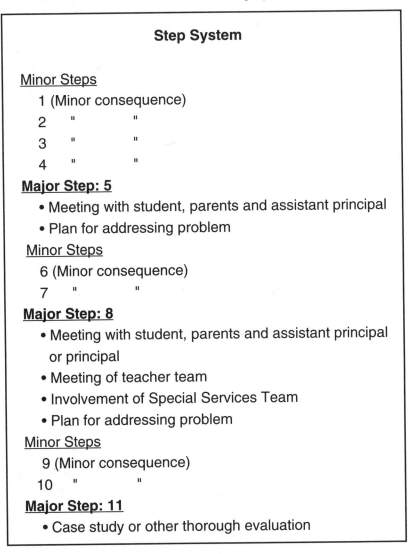

Step System

<u>Minor Steps</u>
   1 (Minor consequence)
   2   "   "
   3   "   "
   4   "   "

<u>Major Step: 5</u>
   • Meeting with student, parents and assistant principal
   • Plan for addressing problem

<u>Minor Steps</u>
   6 (Minor consequence)
   7   "   "

<u>Major Step: 8</u>
   • Meeting with student, parents and assistant principal
     or principal
   • Meeting of teacher team
   • Involvement of Special Services Team
   • Plan for addressing problem

<u>Minor Steps</u>
   9 (Minor consequence)
   10 "   "

<u>Major Step: 11</u>
   • Case study or other thorough evaluation

The above system is a general plan for discipline, which can be modified by each school according to its needs. It is also a good idea for the plan to be explained in the beginning of the school year and published in some kind of student handbook. The idea of "progressing" on the step system is itself something of a deterrent to students.

Students can go back "down" on the Step System by going ten school days without any incident occurring. A student at Step 9, for example, can go back to Step 8. The interventions listed above, of course, do not kick in as the student goes back down. Most kids like the idea of this kind of positive reinforcement, and it also reduces their vulnerability to more "intrusive" interventions. Although it is beyond the scope of this book, a step system like this has been also used successfully at the high school level.

Part VI

Your Child's
Self-Esteem

25

10 Steps for Building Self-Esteem

E very parent wants to help his or her children have good self-esteem. Realistic and positive self-esteem is essential throughout life to maintain a good mood, assert oneself with confidence, get along with others, and even keep physically healthy. How can parents make sure that their children will think well of themselves?

This task is obviously easier said than done—and you don't have total control over the matter—but here are ten important steps that can help you go a long way.

1. Get Real!

"Get real" means two things. The first is that a child's self-esteem will never be based on some kind of gimmick. Self-respect will be based on the child's entire life. A little bit of this or that "self-esteem technique" won't even scratch the surface if the youngster's whole life is a disaster. Sometimes, reading articles or books about self-esteem, you begin to get the feeling there's some way of tricking a child into thinking well of himself in spite of the fact that he's flunking in school, has no friends and is a major pain to manage at home. It isn't true.

Second—like it or not—you don't have total control over how your kids turn out or over their ultimate level of self-esteem. You can do the best you can, but it's important to realize that many other factors contribute to their development. For example, innate physical and mental capabilities are strongly influenced by heredity (you don't control the genes you give your kids). Children are also influenced by others outside the family, by their schools and teachers, and by the times in which they live. Just plain good and bad luck can play a large role.

Kids, therefore, are not like putty in your hands.

Why is it important to realize this? Because your self-esteem as a parent has a lot to do with how your kids are doing. If you are expecting the impossible of yourself, of course, you will suffer. You will also run the risk of putting pressure on your children to accomplish what may not be possible.

2. Manage the Two "Curses"

It sometimes seems that whoever designed us as parents did the job backwards. What we tend to naturally think and what we tend to naturally do very often are unrealistic or negative or both. The thinking curse and the action curse are biological and ingrained. The first makes our thinking overly perfectionistic, and the second can be summed up in the phrase, "Angry parents make noise, happy ones keep quiet."

If you do ten things in the course of a day, and you handle nine correctly while you mess up one, which do you think about at the end of the day? Most people stew about the thing they messed up. They take for granted what they did right and forget about it.

But forget about a mistake? No way. For some reason we just seem to be much more impressed by what goes wrong than by what goes right. Isn't this what the news on TV is all about?

Unfortunately, evaluating one's own behavior with this "news-caster" mentality has a predictable effect on self-esteem, and it certainly isn't a good one. This natural tendency toward magnified self-criticism makes people discouraged and even depressed.

What does all this have to do with my kids, you ask? If you think this way about yourself, you will tend to treat other family members in the same way. You will be more impressed by the mistakes and failings of your spouse and your children than you will by their good points.

This kind of thinking leads to the second curse, which affects the way we act. If you are more preoccupied with the negative aspects of your children's behavior, you will probably reflect that orientation in what you talk about. The idea that "angry parents make noise" while "happy parents keep quiet" is based on more than just thinking.

Anger motivates action (including talking), while contentment does not. Anger produces the "fight or flight" response, which revs up the body to do something. So when the kids irritate you, you are likely to come up with some "fighting words." Yet, when the children are playing happily with no problems, you are not likely to say anything.

What is one to do about the two curses? First of all, remember that your kids do much more good than bad—they are basically good little people. Second, let your speech and actions reflect that fact by paying attention to the nine other self-esteem steps mentioned here.

3. Good Discipline Is Basic

Unless you know what you're doing when it comes to disciplining the kids and maintaining order in the home, none of the other steps mentioned here will do much good. In fact, you won't even feel like doing any of the rest of them. Good discipline is what *1-2-3 Magic* is all about.

If you don't have your discipline act together, the kids will constantly have you feeling overwhelmed with anger and resentment. You will be yelling and screaming—or perhaps even worse. But kids are just kids. They are erratic and still learning what's what. They are supposed to frustrate you on a regular basis. If you can't take this aggravation more or less in stride and handle it, you will communicate to them that they are nothing more than a pain in the neck to you. It doesn't take a rocket scientist to figure out what this message will do to their self-esteem.

In addition, research has shown that erratic discipline tends to produce hostile and erratic behavior in children, which furthers a downward spiral of self-esteem.

Here's a quick check on your home discipline. First ask yourself, "What are the three biggest problems I'm having with my kids?" Perhaps your response is sibling rivalry, whining and bedtime. Next ask yourself what your method is for dealing with each of these problems. If you can't answer fairly quickly, or if your answer is you're not sure, or if what you really do is some version of arguing, yelling, nagging or hitting, then you're in trouble.

And you also, apparently, didn't read this book! Better review it and get started. By the way, if those are your problems, look up sibling rivalry in Chapter 8, whining in Chapter 10, and bedtime in Chapter 18.

4. Treat Any Problems

The development of many children is impaired by emotional, behavioral or physical problems that can make life much more of a challenge. Anxiety disorders, learning disabilities, Attention Deficit Disorder, asthma or physical handicaps can make kids feel different, hinder their ability to perform normally, and lower self-esteem. Obviously, helping a child deal with these problems as well as possible is critical to the psychological welfare of affected youngsters.

Yet many parents hold back on doing something for any number of reasons. Perhaps they are not sure if there is a problem. Or the child isn't requesting help and may even fight the idea of seeing a doctor. Parents also feel—perhaps correctly—that the very act of "seeking help for a problem" has a negative effect on self-esteem.

Such thinking isn't realistic and is only looking at the short-term. Kids rarely ask to see anyone for these kinds of problems, but they only get one chance to grow up. A good rule of thumb is this: if you have been worrying for more than one year about the possibility that your child suffers from a particular kind of problem and you haven't checked it out, it's past the time to do something. If you check it out and there is a problem, you can do something about it. If you find out there is no problem, you can stop worrying.

5. Positive Reinforcement

Kids need positive, supportive comments from you on a frequent and regular basis. (See the first Start behavior tactic in Chapter 14.)

How about establishing a "quota system"? Each day, be sure to give every other person in the family (including your spouse!) three positive comments, such as:

"Good job!"
"Thanks for getting that for me."
"That was really hard for you, but you did it."
"I think you handled that very well."

These statements don't take much time, but they will be remembered and can make a big difference to someone's self-esteem.

6. Shared Fun

A famous psychologist once said, "Show me two people who have fun together on a regular basis and I'll show you a good relationship." Being together in the same place at the same time and enjoying the same thing is almost the essence of what some people like to refer to as "bonding."

The fun doesn't have to be fancy or expensive. It could be a vacation, but it could also be watching a movie at home, shopping, playing baseball, going out for a hamburger, or just talking. Knowing you're going to do something fun with a child helps you get along better beforehand. After the event is over, the pleasant memories help you get along better. While this is especially true for the older kids (8 to 12), the little ones (2 to 3) won't remember much.

As the parent, try to find something you enjoy too, not just something you tolerate for the sake of your child. And while you're out having a good time, don't talk about problems unless the child wants to. Can you manage doing something fun once a week for at least one hour?

Fun with the entire family is good and necessary. What many parents don't like to hear, however, is that the kind of fun that means the most to the kids is one-on-one. One parent with one child. The bad news here is that it takes more time if you have more than one child. The good news is that the lack of sibling rivalry also makes it more pleasant for Mom or Dad.

7. Plain Old Affection

Verbal and nonverbal expressions of affection also help a child feel good about himself. Affection put in words is very similar to positive reinforcement, so make sure it is tailored to the child. Some kids like the more obvious kinds, and some kids prefer the more subdued and subtle. The little ones may like to sit on your lap for a while. The older ones may prefer a hug or a pat on the back.

8. Expertise Building

Any child feels good about being good at something. Helping a youngster find something that he can excel at and nurturing his interest over time can work wonders for self-esteem. Perhaps the child is good at one sport (or several). Maybe she likes computers or he enjoys music. How about reading or writing or school itself? It's always nice if the child's area of expertise is something that no other child in the family is into, but this, of course, isn't always possible.

Nurturing a child's interests and skills does not mean shoving something down his throat. Nurturing does mean phone calls, chauffeuring, dollars and watching him do his thing!

9. Non-Evaluation

Parents were put on earth for a lot of reasons: to guide their kids, nurture them, give them a sense of values, and keep them out of trouble. Yet kids don't need to have their parents riding them all the time.

The 1-2-3 works very well in managing Stop behavior, but the power of the 1-2-3 can be abused. A parent could use it to pick and pick a child to death. Try to decide beforehand what kinds of things you will count. Try also to notice how much your counting changes depending on your mood. Some change may be inevitable, but too much variability will confuse the kids.

It's nice to have quiet times when no one is being evaluated.

10. Active Listening

The last point about fostering self-esteem in children is important enough to merit its own chapter. Active listening may sound rather fancy or even "shrink-like," but it's a great way to get along and one of the most potent ways to help your kids feel confident about themselves.

26

Active Listening

Your ten-year-old son, Tom, comes running in the door after school yelling, "My music teacher's an idiot!" What should you do?

You could count—after all the kid is screaming. But think for a second. He is *not* screaming at you, he *is* upset about something, and you don't know what it is. Your priorities? Give the child some support and find out what happened. His being angry is no crime, and his outburst couldn't be testing and manipulation, because you didn't do anything to frustrate him.

Here is a time for "active listening." The conversation might go something like this:

Tom: "My music teacher's an idiot!"
Mom: "Tell me what happened."
Tom: "She made me sing in front of the whole stupid class, and only one other kid—a girl—had to do it. She didn't care, but all my friends were laughing at me!"
Mom: "What did she make you sing?"
Tom: "I don't know, some stupid religious hymn or some

other completely dumb thing."

Mom: "That must have been awfully embarrassing."

Tom: "I'm going to bomb her car!"

Mom: "Boy, I haven't seen you this mad for a while! So what happened when you had to sing?"

Tom: "She makes me stand in the front of the room, then she plays her idiot piano, and I don't even know the dumb song! I could see Dave was giggling and trying not to laugh. I'd like to see him do it!"

Mom: "So you thought it wasn't very fair for her to make you do it when no one else had to."

Tom: "Yeah. Why are they picking on me all the time? What a dumb school." (Tom leaves to get a snack.)

Active Listening and Self-Esteem

Active listening is a way of talking to someone with sympathy or empathy (the distinction between the two isn't important here). It is very respectful of another's thoughts and feelings, because the listener doesn't just sit there, but instead attempts to see the world through the other person's eyes.

When you are listening to your child, you are—like the mother above—forgetting your own opinions for a while, suspending judgment, and committing yourself to completely understanding how the child saw a particular situation (you don't have to agree with him). In our example Mom is not thinking that her son is being disrespectful or that he caused the trouble. Nor is she formulating her own response.

Active listening, therefore, tries to accomplish two things: 1) to understand what another person is saying and thinking—from his or her point of view, and 2) to communicate back and check your understanding with the person doing the talking. The listener is an active participant in the conversation, not someone who just sits and nods from time to time.

Active listening is not easy, but it can be mastered. Once you get past the point of feeling artificial, "parrot-like" or too passive, you can sometimes pleasantly knock the kids right off their feet. And it is an excellent way to begin any lengthy, serious conversation.

How Do You Do Active Listening?

First, get yourself in the proper frame of mind: "I'm going to hear this kid out—even if it kills me—and find out exactly what he thinks and feels about what's going on." Next, several different things can be done, and once you get used to them the whole process will feel very natural. These include openers, nonjudgmental questions, reflecting feelings, and perception checks or summaries.

In the example above, here's where these "tactics" appeared:

Tom: "My music teacher's an idiot!"
Mom: "Tell me what happened." (Opener)
Tom: "She made me sing in front of the whole stupid class, and
only one other kid—a girl—had to do it. She didn't care, but
all my friends were laughing at me!"
Mom: "What did she make you sing?" (Question)
Tom: "I don't know, some stupid religious hymn or some
other completely dumb thing."
Mom: "That must have been awfully embarrassing."
(Reflecting feeling)
Tom: "I'm going to bomb her car!"
Mom: "Boy, I haven't seen you this mad for a while!
(Reflecting feeling)
"So what happened when you had to sing?" (Question)
Tom: "She makes me stand in the front of the room, then she
plays her idiot piano, and I don't even know the dumb song!
I could see Dave was giggling and trying not to laugh. I'd like
to see him do it!"
Mom: "So you thought it wasn't very fair for her to make you
do it when no one else had to." (Check/Summary)
Tom: "Yeah. Why are they picking on me all the time? What a
dumb school." (Tom leaves to get something to eat.)

Openers

Start with what are called "openers"—brief comments or questions designed to elicit further information from your child. These comments often require self-control, and are especially difficult when you are caught off guard. They may also appear incredibly passive or wimpy to you, but remember that active listening must precede any problem-solving discussion. If discipline or other action is necessary, worry about that after you've gotten the facts.

Openers can be very simple:

"Oh?"
"Wow!"
"Yeah."
"What?"

An opener can be anything that communicates that you are ready and willing to listen sympathetically, including nonverbal behavior, such as sitting down next to the youngster or putting down the paper to look at him.

Nonjudgmental Questions

Following openers, more questions are often necessary. To be effective, these must not be loaded or judgmental.

Here are some bad questions:

"Why did you do a stupid thing like that?"
"What on earth were you thinking?!"
"What's your problem today?"
"Why are you bugging me now about this?"

These questions will inspire argument or silence.

Here are some better questions that might keep the talk going as well as elicit more understanding:

"What do you think made you do that?"
"What was going through your mind at the time?"
"Sounds like something's bothering you today?"
"Why are you worried about this now?"

In print alone, of course, we can't describe the tone of voice that should accompany these questions, but it should be readily apparent that any of the above can be ruined by a sarcastic, angry, belittling, conde-scending or totally smart-alec tone of voice.

Reflecting Feelings

If you are going to tell someone that you think you understand him, try to let him know that you can imagine how he must have felt under the circumstances he's describing to you. Sometimes the older kids will tell you that you sound a bit like a shrink. If that's the case, just say, "Sorry, but I'm just trying to make sure I understand what you're talking about."

In the example above, Mom reflected feelings back at two points:

"That must have been awfully embarrassing."
"Boy, I haven't seen you this mad for a while!"

Other examples of reflecting feelings might include:

"You really sound bummed out about that."
"That must have really been fun!"
"You were pretty upset with me."

Reflecting feelings does a couple of things. It lets the child know that whatever he is feeling is OK (it's what he sometimes does about it that can be right or wrong). This response reinforces self-esteem and also helps diffuse the feeling so it is not acted out somewhere else. You can bet that if Tom's mother had first said, "That's no way to talk about your teachers!" his anger would have been immediately redirected at her.

Perception Checks

The name may sound fancy, but the idea is simple. From time to time during a talk, it is helpful to check out with the other person whether or not you are "catching his drift" or really getting a good idea of what he's saying. This kind of comment lets you know whether you're understand-ing the child correctly, but it also has a second purpose: it tells the child that you're really listening to what he's saying and that you're really trying to see the world for a moment through his eyes.

Examples of checks or summaries might be:

"Sounds like you're saying that our rules for chores favor
  your sister."
"You felt it was your worst day at school this year."
"You're feeling like the new homework arrangement we
  started is working a lot better."
"You wish I weren't gone so much so we could do more
  together?"

Active listening is also an attitude. Your attitude, not your child's. It's the attitude of sincerely trying to figure out what someone else is thinking even if you don't agree or even if it drives you nuts. This, of course, is a different kind of job if you're talking to a two-year-old or a ten-year-old. Either way it's a great self-esteem builder.

You'll also find that if you listen well you can learn a lot about what your children think about life.

27

Active Listening
and Counting

In Chapter 5 we described counting and how to use it if the kids are giving you a hard time. Then in Chapter 26 we discussed how active listening helps diffuse negative emotions. How in the world is a parent supposed to know when to listen and when to count?

If you active listened *all the time*, you wouldn't be any kind of a disciplinarian. Active listening, by itself, has nothing to do with setting limits and enforcing rules. Imagine this scene:

"Mom—you idiot! My best T-shirt's still in the wash!"
"You're feeling pretty frustrated with me."

This parent's response is overly nice and also inappropriate. The child's disrespect is way out of proportion to the situation and should be confronted.

On the other hand, if you counted *all the time* whenever the kids were upset, you wouldn't be a very understanding parent. Your kids would correctly perceive you as only an instrument of discipline—or worse.

Imagine this common summertime scene:

"I'm bored."
"That's 1."

That's also a pretty insensitive and unnecessary response. Your kids certainly won't want to talk to you very often!

When to count and when to listen? Sometimes it's pretty clear, but often it's not a very easy decision. Here are some guidelines.

If They're Not Upset with *You*

If the child is upset about something that didn't have anything to do with you, it is probably time to active listen. This behavior couldn't be Testing and Manipulation directed at you, because you didn't do anything to frustrate the child.

You're in the family room, for example, and seven-year-old Jim comes running in from outside yelling:

"THOSE GUYS ARE JERKS!"
"Who's that, Jim?"
"The kids across the street—they won't let me go in their yard."
"Why not?"
"I don't know. They're just morons."
"Boy, you sound really upset!"
"Yeah, I'm not playing with those creeps."
"That sounds like a good idea."

Dad doesn't count the yelling. The problem occurred outside and didn't have anything to do with him, so he figures a little active listening may diffuse the situation.

Or, back to the old summertime refrain (Janie, 10):

"I'm bored."
"You're not having a very good day, huh?"
"No. There's nothing to do."
"You try, but you can't think of anything fun at all?"

"Nope. Can we go get that book I wanted?"
"I've got to go to the mall, anyway. Let's do it."
"All right!"

Mom here doesn't get trapped into making seven suggestions that will be shot down one by one. Her daughter is not feeling too good, but this isn't Badgering or any other type of manipulation. Time for a little sympathy. If the two of them can work out something to do, fine. If not, see the next example.

The Upset Switches *to You*

Sometimes the kids will start out upset by something else, but then their frustration will switch to the parent. In that case you can still try active listening, but you had better be ready to count.

Janie's situation above is a little tricky. What if Mom doesn't want to do anything or can't go out?

"I'm bored."
"You're not having a very good day, huh?"
"No. There's nothing to do."
"You try, but you can't think of anything fun at all?"
"Nope. Can we go get that new book I wanted?"
"I can't, honey."
"Aw, why not?"
"I've got things to do here."
"What do you have to do?"
"It doesn't make any difference. Plenty. Look, why don't you
    call Megan and see if she wants to do something. I could
    maybe pick her up."
"If you can pick her up, why can't you take me to get my book."
"Better drop it, Janie, or we're going to counting."
"You don't let me do ANYTHING!"
"That's 1."
"THAT'S ONE FOR YOU, TOO!"
"That's 2."
"Oh for pete's sake." (Janie leaves.)

Here Mom tries active listening, but it doesn't defuse the situation. Janie puts the hit on her to be the local entertainment committee. Mom can't produce the desired services, so Janie gets into Badgering, Martyrdom and Intimidation. Mom catches herself getting verbally involved in the impossible, and starts counting.

Discuss Problems, Count Attacks

What if the kids are upset with you in the first place? This situation gets even trickier. It depends partly upon how they approach you. In general the rule, "Discuss Problems, Count Attacks," applies.

> "Mom—you idiot—my best T-shirt's still in the wash!"
> "It was filthy-dirty, and that's no way to talk to anybody,
>   young man. That's 1."
> "I NEEDED TO WEAR IT THIS AFTERNOON!"
> "That's 2."
> "Jerk!"
> "Take 10, and add 10 more for the mouth."

An attack from the start. Mom did very well. Many parents would give an immediate "3" for the "idiot" remark.

Some things are pretty much attacks, but if a parent uses a little active listening, the emotion may be diffused and things can work out. Mark is ten:

> "Why are you making me do this stupid homework now!?"
> "Homework's a real bummer, isn't it?"
> "Oh, brother." (Mark starts his homework with a sigh.)

Here the active listening helped diffuse the unpleasant emotion so the child didn't act on it. Keep the 1-2-3 ready in your back pocket, though, because you may not always be so lucky:

> "Why are you making me do this stupid homework now?!"
> "Homework's a real bummer, isn't it?"
> "Yeah, I hate it!"

"Boy, you really don't like it, do you?"
"I could be rollerblading with Jason."
"You'd really prefer to be outside playing."
"DON'T JUST SAY BACK EVERYTHING I SAY!"
"That's 1."

Remarkable presence of mind on the part of this parent.

So what's the basic rule? Be ready to discuss problems. But if the child's part of the discussion becomes an attack in the form of Badgering, Threats, Intimidation, whining or some Physical tactic, count.

28

The Payoff

Now that you know what the 1-2-3 is all about, it's time to get started. You have lots of company. To date the 1-2-3 has been used by hundreds of thousands of parents in all 50 states—not to mention a number of foreign countries. It has also been used successfully in schools, preschools and daycare centers. Some community mental health centers integrate the 1-2-3 with their evaluation and treatment of children's problems. In one mental health center, for example, parents of young children who call for an appointment attend a two-part 1-2-3 workshop before they ever see a therapist. After completing this brief training program, approximately 80 per cent of the parents do not feel they need further services.

1-2-3 Magic is known for producing results. It works—and it often works in a very short period of time. No magic. Just the logical, consistent application of certain basic principles to the *nth* degree.

What can you expect if you decide to use the 1-2-3 at home? You can expect a more peaceful household, with a lot less arguing and fewer angry moments. There will be more time for fun, and affection will come more easily. The self-esteem of your children will improve, and so will your self-esteem as a parent, because you will be more effective, more in control, and you will know you are handling things correctly. If you are a teacher, you will feel more confident, more in control of your class, and you will have more time for instruction.

What it boils down to is this: how do you want to spend your time with your children? You can spend it like this:

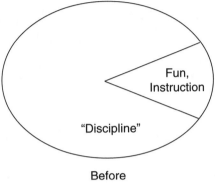

Before
1-2-3 MAGIC

Here the kids are driving you crazy most of the time. You are caught up in frequent but futile "attempts" at discipline. There is little time to enjoy the children, educate them or even like them.

On the other hand, you can spend your time like this:

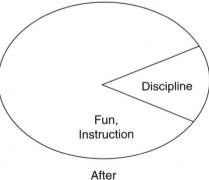

After
1-2-3 MAGIC

In this situation the proper perspective has been established. Sanity is restored by the 1-2-3, which makes discipline crisp, gentle and efficient. There's less arguing and yelling, and in this more peaceful atmosphere affection can unfold naturally. Everyone's self-esteem benefits.

Parents have often said the 1-2-3 works "like magic." That's where we got the title. What do the kids say about it? Many children say they don't like it, and the reason, of course, is that they are not getting their way as much as they did before.

But—more importantly—many more children have said they like the 1-2-3. When asked why, they say, "Because Mom and Dad don't yell so much." That's a very meaningful statement. It's essential for parents to be in charge of their homes, but it's also crucial that they do this in a way that is not emotionally or physically harmful to their children.

So, it's time to get going with the Kickoff Conversation. Begin by using the 1-2-3 on Stop behavior: do the counting for a week or two to get things under control, and then add the Start behavior techniques. Don't be naive. Get yourself ready for some good old-fashioned Testing and Manipulation.

The 1-2-3 works—*if you do it*. Things could be quite different at your house—or in your classroom—in a very short period of time. That's an exciting thought! You'll have kids who listen and children whom you can enjoy.